WHY THE SACKCLOTH?

WHY THE SACKCLOTH?

Charles A Thompson

WHY THE SACKCLOTH?
Published by CT Art & Design, LLC
PO Box 9623
Brea, CA 92822 USA
charlesathompson.com

Library of Congress Control Number: 2026908829
ISBN: 979-8-9955077-0-3
EISBN: 979-8-9955077-1-0

First Edition 2026

Printed in the United States of America.

Contents

Chapter 1:

The Liquid Language

THE CURSE OF THE CRY BABY

Growing up, I was a cry baby. There is no polite way to say it, and there was certainly no polite way to experience it. Sensitivity was not viewed as a gift; it was a target. I felt everything. If the tone of a room shifted, I felt it in my chest. If someone looked at me with a hint of disapproval, I felt the hair rising in my neck. If I saw someone struggling, or a friend treated unfairly, the reaction wasn't just mental, it was physical.

My body would betray me. The lump would form in the

throat; that painful, jagged stone that refuses to be swallowed. The eyes would burn, and then, the humiliation would begin. The water would spill over.

I hated it. I viewed my own lacrimal glands as a defect in my manufacturing. I saw other boys, and later other men, who seemed to be made of stone. Words bounced off them. Tragedy seemed to strike them and slide away like rain on a waxed car. They were "strong." I was "weak" or "feminine."

I remember lying in bed at night, staring at the ceiling, praying a prayer that terrifies me now in retrospect. I would pray: "Lord, please harden my heart."

I wanted the callous. I wanted the scar tissue. I thought that if I could just kill the sensitivity, I could survive the harshness of people's words. I thought that if I could stop the flow of this liquid, I would finally be stronger. I did not know then what I know now.

I did not know that I was asking God to sever our line of communication.

I did not know that the sensitivity I despised was actually a receiver designed by the Creator to detect His presence. I did not know that the tears I wiped away in shame were actually a sophisticated biological technology, a liquid language, that my body was speaking when my mouth ran out of words.

We live in a world that tells us to "suck it up. " We are taught that composure is the highest form of dignity. But the God of the Bible is not a God of composure; He is a God of connection, and He designed the human vessel with a pressure valve that is essential for our survival.

We are the crying babies of the universe. We are finite, fragile, and easily overwhelmed. And God, like a good parent, is not looking down at us with disgust, implying our pain is a mere inconvenience. He is looking at us with the wisdom of a physician, telling us to let it out because it's necessary.

We think we are doing God a favor when we hold it together. In reality, He is commanding us to fall apart. He is like a parent telling a toddler, "You need to brush your teeth." The toddler thinks it's a chore; the parent knows it's hygiene.

This book is about the hygiene of the soul. And it begins with understanding the machinery of the eye.

THE ARCHITECTURE OF THE VESSEL

The vessel itself is a revelation of God's design. To the

naked eye, a tear is a simple thing. It is a drop of saline. It looks like water. It tastes like salt. If you were to wipe one from your cheek and place it under a microscope, it would appear unremarkable.

The simplicity of the tear is an illusion. If you were to take that same drop of fluid and subject it to a chemical analysis, or freeze it and photograph its crystallized structure, you would discover that crying is not a singular biological event. The human body is a precision instrument, and it does not waste energy producing generic fluids. It produces specific tools for specific jobs.

Science tells us that you do not cry one type of tear. You cry three.

Tucked inside the bony ridge of your brow, just above the outer corner of your eye, is the lacrimal gland. It is roughly the size and shape of an almond. This is the factory floor.

For most of your day, this gland is operating on a low hum, a background setting that you are completely unaware of. It is part of a larger, complex system known as the *lacrimal apparatus*. This system consists of secretory glands, a distribution mechanism (the eyelids), and a drainage system (the puncta and nasolacrimal ducts).

Every time you blink, roughly fifteen to twenty times a minute, your eyelids sweep across the surface of your cornea like windshield wipers. But unlike the wipers on a car, which merely push water away, your eyelids are painting. With every closure, they spread a microscopic, perfectly even layer of fluid across the surface of the eye. This tear is called the **Basal Tear.**

Basal tears are the architects of your vision. Without them, the cornea would starve for oxygen and dry out within minutes, becoming opaque and useless. The basal tear is the life-support system for your sight. It is a three-layer film: mucus to stick to the eye, water to hydrate it, and oil to seal it so it does not evaporate.

This layer is constant. It is the "daily bread" of the ocular system. It represents God's sustaining grace. This is the invisible work He does to keep our vision clear, even when we are not asking for it.

The factory has a second tear. It is designed not just for maintenance, but for defense. Imagine you are standing in a kitchen, slicing an onion. The moment the blade breaks into the vegetable, a gas is released. It hits the moisture of your eye and turns into mild sulfuric acid.

Your body perceives this immediately as an assault. The sensory nerves on the surface of your cornea send a distress signal screaming toward the brainstem. The message is simple and urgent: *Help.*

The brain does not hesitate. It bypasses the emotional centers entirely. This is not a matter for the heart, but for survival. It sends a command back to the lacrimal gland to open the floodgates. This second type of tear is the **Reflex Tear**.

Reflex tears are the soldiers. They are released in massive volume. Their purpose is not to nourish, but to flush. They are a biological fire hose aimed at a specific threat like dust, smoke, sand, or chemical fumes. In this case it is the sulfuric acid caused by the onion. They flush out the invaders.

If these were the only two types of tears humans produced, our biology would be easy to explain. We would be efficient, survival-oriented mammals, possessing a system to keep our eyes wet and a system to wash them clean.

We are not just mammals. We are souls that possess a third gear that activates not when we are physically attacked, but when we are spiritually overwhelmed.

THE MYSTERY OF THE THIRD TEAR

In the 19th century, Charles Darwin, the father of evolutionary biology, famously dismissed emotional weeping as "purposeless." To the scientific mind of the Victorian era, the tear was a physiological accident, a useless secretion that served no function in the survival of the fittest. A gazelle does not weep when it is hunted and a wolf does not shed tears when it is hungry. Why would the human animal waste precious hydration and obscure its own vision in moments of crisis? Darwin was wrong. The tear is not an accident, but the answer. This brings us to the **Emotional Tear**.

In the early 1980s, a biochemist named Dr. William Frey II at the St. Paul-Ramsey Medical Center began to ask a question that changed the way we view grief. He wondered if the tears shed during emotional distress were chemically different from those shed due to physical irritation.

He designed a study where he collected reflex tears, by exposing volunteers to fresh onions, and emotional tears, by showing them sad movies. Then he analyzed the chemical composition of the fluid.

Frey found that the emotional tears were chemically

denser. They contained significantly higher levels of proteins, specifically, a twenty to twenty-four percent increase in protein concentration.

It was not just protein in general. It was specific cargo. Frey found that emotional tears carried hormones that were largely absent or found in much lower concentrations in the reflex tears.

The lacrimal gland, when triggered by the heart rather than the onion, changes the recipe.

THE CARGO: DETOXIFYING THE SOUL

What is inside an emotional tear?

First, Frey found Adrenocorticotropic Hormone (ACTH). This is the trigger for the stress response. When you are anxious or traumatized, your pituitary gland pumps out ACTH, which travels to your adrenal glands and tells them to release cortisol. Cortisol is the stress hormone that keeps you awake, tense, and ready to fight. Frey found that emotional tears are loaded with ACTH.

When you cry because you are stressed, you are not just letting out emotion. You are literally excreting the chemical build-up of stress. You are dumping the trigger mechanism out of your body.

Second, he found Manganese. Manganese is a mineral that affects mood. In trace amounts, it is necessary, but when manganese levels in the brain get too high, it becomes a neurotoxin. Clinical overexposure to manganese is linked to anxiety, nervousness, irritability, and aggression. It destabilizes the emotional regulation of the brain.

Frey discovered that the concentration of manganese in emotional tears was thirty times higher than the concentration in blood serum.

The lacrimal gland is capable of concentrating this specific, mood-destabilizing mineral and expelling it from your body at a rate thirty times faster than your kidneys can filter it from your blood.

This gives a whole new meaning to the phrase "crying it out." You are not just crying out a feeling, you are crying out a poison.

This is the biological purpose of the Sackcloth state. When we enter into lament, when we allow ourselves to weep, we are engaging in a biological detox system. We are lowering the toxicity of our brains.

This explains why, after a "good cry," we often feel a sense of lightness or relief. The situation has not changed. The loss is still real. The heartbreak is still there, but the chemical pressure has been vented. The "issues in the tissues" have been flushed. This is why I call it **The Liquid Language.**

Language is a system of encoding meaning. We usually use sound waves (speech) or symbols (writing) to transmit what is inside of us to the outside world. Spoken language has limits.

Have you ever been in so much pain that you could not speak? The mechanism of the brain that controls speech is the Broca's Area, and it actually shuts down during high-stress trauma. You literally can not find the words. You are mute with grief.

In that moment, if you did not have a secondary language, you would be trapped in your own skull. You would explode.

So, God gave us a liquid language. He gave us a way to speak when words fail. He gave us a way to offload the pain without needing a vocabulary.

THE GOD WHO UNDERSTANDS

The Bible, thousands of years before biochemistry, understood this mechanism. In Psalm 56:8, David, a man who spent years running for his life, hiding in caves, and facing betrayal, writes one of the most intimate verses in Scripture:

> *You keep track of all my sorrows. You have collected all my tears in your bottle. Are they not in your record?*
>
> ***-Psalm 56:8***

For centuries, we have read this as a poetic metaphor. If you look closer, David calls God a "Collector."

Why do you collect things? You collect things that have value. You collect things that contain information.

David is suggesting that God does not let the liquid language fall to the ground and evaporate. He catches it. He understands it.

If tears are filled with biological data like hormones, proteins, minerals, then they are a transmission of data. They are a code, God translates those tears to words.

> *In the same way, the Spirit helps us in our*

> *weakness. We do not know what we ought to pray for, but the Spirit himself intercedes for us through wordless groans.*
>
> ***- Romans 8:26***

When I fought tears, praying for a hard heart, I thought my tears were a sign that I was broken. I thought I was sending static on the line, but in reality, I was sending the purest, most honest signal a human being can send.

Spoken prayers can be faked. We can use religious jargon. We can say, "God, I trust you," while our hearts are terrified. We can perform for the audience around us (as we will see in Matthew 6).

But you cannot fake the chemistry of a tear. A tear is pure truth. It is the distilled essence of what is actually happening inside your nervous system.

When we cry to God, we are bypassing our own ability to lie. We are bypassing our own need to sound spiritual. We are handing Him the bottle and saying, "Here. This is what hurts. I can't say it, but here is the chemistry of it."

And God says, "I can read this."

THE COMMAND TO BRUSH YOUR TEETH

Why does God command us to lament? Why does scripture tell us that *"The heart of the wise is in the house of mourning"* (Ecclesiastes 7:4)? Why does Jesus say, *"Blessed are those who mourn"*?

Is it because God is a sadist? Is it because He enjoys seeing His children in pain?

No. It is because He is a Designer.

He knows that we live in a fallen world. He knows that we are absorbing trauma, rejection, and stress every single day. He knows that the manganese of life is building up in our systems.

If we do not release it, we become toxic. The toxic heart takes unprocessed grief and hardens into bitterness. The toxic body takes unreleased stress and turns into hypertension, autoimmune disease, and ulcers. The toxic spirit takes a heart that can not cry and eventually it can not feel God.

We tend to view God's commands as burdens. We read Fast, Give, Pray, and Lament, and we hear a chore list. We think we are doing these things for Him, to prove our loyalty.

God is self-sufficient. He does not need our fasting to be

full. He does not need our money to be rich. He does not need our tears to know what is happening. He commands these things for us.

Imagine a toddler screaming because their parents are forcing them to brush their teeth. The toddler thinks, "Why do I have to do this?"

The parent is not enforcing a rule for the sake of power. The parent knows about tooth decay. The parent knows that sugar left on the enamel will rot the tooth, reach the nerve, and cause agony. The brushing is a preventative grace.

We are the toddlers. We want to live our best life. We want to be justified. Tears equate to a toxic environment, so we run from tears like the plague.

God, our Father, stands there with the toothbrush of Lament, saying, "You need to do this. You need to get the rot out. If you leave that pain in there, it will eat you alive."

The disciplines we will explore in this book are **Lament, Fasting, Giving, and Prayer.** This is the hygiene of an abundant life.

Lament flushes the emotional toxin.

Fasting flushes the distraction toxin.

Giving flushes the greed/fear toxin.

Prayer flushes the anxiety toxin.

When we practice these, we are not earning God's love. We are clearing the static on the line. We are scrubbing the vessel clean so that it can hold the one thing that matters: **His Presence.**

In the Garden of Eden, there were no tears. This was not just because there was no death. It was because there was no barrier. Adam and Eve walked in the cool of the day with God. They were fully known and fully safe.

We live in the gap between the Garden we lost and the Second Coming. In this gap, the static is loud. The pain is real. The temptation to have a stone heart so that you are numb to the things of this world is overwhelming.

A stone cannot feel. A stone cannot love. A stone cannot hold the Spirit of God. Let us stop apologizing for our tears. Let us stop running from the sackcloth. Let us embrace the liquid language. It is time to brush your teeth.

Chapter 2:
The Toxic Load

We live in a culture that equates the emotionless as strong. We pin medals on the people who can take a hit and keep walking. We elect leaders who show no emotion. We look up to the stoic father who buries his grief in his work, and the resilient mother who carries the weight of the entire family without ever breaking a sweat.

We call this strength. Biology calls it chronic inflammation.

We have a fundamental misunderstanding of what trauma does to the human body. We tend to think of grief, betrayal, and stress as mental events as abstractions that haunt our thoughts but leave our flesh untouched. We think that if we can just keep a positive mindset, or give it to God (by ignoring it), our bodies will remain unaffected.

The body is not a machine. It is a chemical plant. Every time you experience a stressor, like a rejection, a fear, or a loss, your body produces a specific chemical payload. It mobilizes energy. It creates matter.

The laws of physics tell us that matter can not be created or destroyed. It can only change form.

So, when you refuse to cry, where does the matter go? When you refuse to speak this Liquid Language, where do the manganese, the ACTH, and the cortisol go?

They do not vanish. They settle. They seep into the fascia of your muscles. They corrode the lining of your stomach. They harden the walls of your arteries. They become what somatic therapists call "The Issues in the Tissues."

In this chapter, we are going to look at the high cost of the tearless life. We are going to explore why certain communities are dying younger, not just because of what they eat, but because of what they hold. We are going to compare the ancient wisdom of the Sackcloth to the modern tragedy of the Cubicle.

PART I: THE PHYSIOLOGY OF BETRAYAL

To understand why we are breaking down, we have to look at how the human body processes a threat. In order to do this, we need to correct a common misconception.

We often hear that modern life is more stressful than ancient life, or conversely, that the biblical life was harder because of lions and starvation. When it comes to emotional trauma, the human experience has been consistent.

Let's create a comparison. Let's look at two men, separated by three thousand years of history, experiencing the exact same event of **The False Accusation.**

The Ancient Man (1000 BC) Imagine an Israelite man living in the court of Saul. He has served faithfully. A rival, someone he trusted, starts a whisper campaign against him. He is accused of treason. He is accused of stealing from the treasury.

He cannot simply kill the accuser because he lacks proof, or perhaps the accuser is powerful. His reputation is destroyed.

His friends stop speaking to him. He is facing social ruin.

The Modern Man (2025 AD) Imagine a corporate executive in New York. He has built his career for twenty years. A rival, someone he mentored, starts a whisper campaign. He is accused of embezzlement and misconduct. He is innocent, but the investigation is humiliating. He is put on leave. His colleagues stop answering his texts. He is cancelled. He faces social ruin.

The Biological Reaction In the split second that both men realize their name is being destroyed, their bodies do the exact same thing.

The Amygdala Hijack: The threat detection center lights up. To a social mammal, "exile from the tribe" is a death threat.

The HPA Axis Activates: The hypothalamus signals the pituitary, which signals the Adrenals.

The Chemical Dump: Cortisol and adrenaline flood the bloodstream.

The Mobilization: The heart rate spikes to 160. Sugar is dumped into the blood for energy. The muscles tense. Digestion stops.

Both men are now in a state of hyper-arousal. They are

vibrating with kinetic energy. They are chemically primed to fight for their lives.

Here is where the story diverges. Here is why the Ancient Man survives, and the Modern Man rots.

The Ancient Response: The Ancient Man lives in a culture that understands the Liquid Language. He knows what to do with the energy of the betrayal.

He tears his clothes. (This is a physical act of controlled violence that discharges kinetic energy). He puts on sackcloth, that rough, scratching goat hair that irritates his skin and grounds him in reality. He goes to the temple. He wails. He screams the words of Psalm 35: *"Contend, Lord, with those who contend with me! ... Malicious witnesses rise up; they ask me of things that I do not know!"*

He fasts. He throws dust in the air. He **Laments**.

He is performing a biological reset. He is burning off the adrenaline. He is excreting the stress chemicals through his tears. He is allowing his community to see his pain, which triggers their support.

At the end of it, he is exhausted, but he is empty. The load is gone.

The Modern Response: The Modern Man lives in a culture that demonizes the Liquid Language. He has the same chemical load. The same 160 heart rate. The same cortisol spike, but he has nowhere to put it.

He has been conditioned to push through. Keep fighting. He does not scream. He cannot tear his suit, that is insane. He cannot weep. Never let anybody see you sweat.

So, what does he do? He hires a lawyer. He sits in a meeting. He is strong. He is composed.

He engages in **Suppression**.

He takes that massive ball of kinetic energy, that "fight or flight" lightning storm, and he swallows it. He forces it down into his belly. He uses his will to clamp down on his biology.

This is the equivalent of revving a car engine to 7,000 RPM while keeping the transmission in neutral and holding down the brake. The car is not moving, but the engine is screaming. The heat is building. The gaskets are about to blow.

Because he does not weep, the manganese stays in his brain increasing his anxiety. Because he does not scream, the adrenaline stays in his muscles, increasing tension. Because he does not process, the cortisol keeps circulating.

Ten years later, the Ancient Man has a scar on his reputation, but his body is healthy. Ten years later, the Modern Man has hypertension, a stomach ulcer, and is prone to sudden fits of rage.

The difference was not the trauma. The difference was the tears. The difference was the release valve.

> *Cast all your anxiety on him because he cares for you.*
>
> ***-I Peter 5:7***

PART II: THE MYTH OF "BEING STRONG"

This biological reality leads us to a difficult conversation about culture, specifically within communities that have had to survive generational trauma.

There is a well-documented health disparity in the United States. Black Americans, for example, suffer from significantly higher rates of hypertension (high blood pressure), heart disease, and stroke compared to other demographics.

For decades, the medical establishment lazily pointed a finger at the "lifestyle." They blamed the food. They blamed the salt. They blamed the soul food.

While diet plays a role, it does not explain the gap. You can take a person with a pristine diet, but if their nervous system is locked in a state of chronic defense, their blood pressure will still kill them.

THE JOHN HENRY EFFECT

Sherman James, an epidemiologist, coined this term based on the folklore of John Henry. The "steel-driving man" who worked so hard to beat the steam engine that he won the race, but his heart exploded, and he died.

The hypothesis is that for marginalized groups, "high-effort coping" becomes a survival strategy. To survive in an environment of systemic racism, economic pressure, and constant scrutiny, you have to work twice as hard. You have to be invulnerable.

Historically, for a Black man or woman in America, showing vulnerability was dangerous. In the era of slavery or Jim Crow, tears could be interpreted as weakness or rebellion. Grief had to be swallowed. Rage had to be hidden behind a mask of compliance. This created a cultural armor. The "Strong Black Woman or " The "Unbreakable Black Man."

This armor was necessary for physical survival in a hostile world. It protected the family. It got the job done. It kept the community standing, but the body keeps the score.

This armor requires a constant, low-level activation of the Sympathetic Nervous System. It requires the body to be always "on guard." It requires the "glottis" to be perpetually tight, holding back the liquid language.

Scientists call the result **weathering**. Just as wind and rain erode a rock over time, the constant bath of stress hormones erodes the telomeres of the DNA. It ages the internal organs faster than the chronological age. This is not a genetic defect, this is a somatic injury. It is the physical result of carrying a load that was meant to be released.

This is where the church has sometimes failed us. We have taken this cultural survival mechanism ("Being Strong") and we have baptized it. We have turned suppression into a spiritual virtue.

We say, "I'm too blessed to be stressed." We say, "Won't He do it!" while our blood pressure is 180/110. We praise the woman who buries her child on Saturday and is leading the choir on Sunday, calling her a warrior.

But is she a warrior? Or is she a casualty?

Is it possible that by applauding her refusal to mourn, by encouraging her to skip the sackcloth, we are cheering her on toward a stroke?

God wants us to be whole, and wholeness requires the release of the toxic load.

> *I have come that they may have life, and have it more abundantly*
>
> ***-John 10:10***

PART III: THE MECHANICS OF THE ROT

Let's get specific about what this load does when it stays inside. What exactly are the "torturers" Jesus spoke of in Matthew 18?

1. The Cardiovascular Assault: When you hold in the Liquid Language (grief/fear), you are keeping your blood vessels constricted. This is the physiology of defense. You are forcing your heart to pump against higher resistance.

Over years, this turbulence damages the inner lining of the arteries (the endothelium). The body repairs these tears with plaque (cholesterol). The plaque hardens. The arteries narrow. The heart has to work even harder.

Eventually, the pressure is too much. The pump fails.

2. The Gastrointestinal Shutdown: The Vagus Nerve connects your brain to your gut. When you are in a state of emotional suppression (holding back tears), the Vagus Nerve signals the gut to slow down. Digestion slows down.

This is why stomach aches are the most common symptom of anxiety in children.

In adults, chronic suppression leads to a gut that never fully rests. The acid balance is thrown off. The microbiome (the good bacteria) is decimated by cortisol. This leads to ulcers, IBS (Irritable Bowel Syndrome) , and systemic inflammation.

We treat the ulcer with medication, but we rarely treat the grief that caused it. We are trying to put out the fire while the arsonist (Suppression) is still in the building.

3. The Immune Collapse: Cortisol is a steroid. In short bursts, it reduces inflammation. When it is chronic because we never cry it out, the immune system becomes "cortisol resistant." It stops listening.

This leads to runaway inflammation. The immune system starts attacking the body's own tissues. This is the root of autoimmune disorders like Lupus, Rheumatoid Arthritis, Hashimoto's.

It is no coincidence that these diseases skyrocket in populations that report high levels of repressed emotion. The body is attacking itself because the trauma is trapped inside the walls.

PART IV: THE HEADACHE OF RESISTANCE

I know this pain personally.

I mentioned in the introduction that I grew up a "cry baby" who learned to stop. I learned to build a dam.

I remember the sensation vividly. Someone would say something cruel. The wave of emotion would rush up from my chest, heading for my eyes. It was a physical force, a tidal wave of the Liquid Language, and I would meet it with an opposing force. My will.

I would clench my jaw. I would tighten my throat muscles. I would stare fixedly at a point on the wall to stop the eyes from blinking.

I was fighting God's design. My body was trying to heal itself (release), and I was trying to protect my ego (suppress).

The result was a specific type of headache. A throbbing, vascular pounding right behind the eyes and at the base of the skull. It felt like my head was in a vise.

I thought it was just a headache. I know now it was the **Friction of Resistance**.

It was the physical heat generated by two opposing nervous systems going to war. The Parasympathetic system was screaming, "Let it go! Reset! Release!" The Sympathetic system was screaming, "Hold it! Don't let them see you break!"

That headache was the sound of the sackcloth being rejected, and the tragedy is, the relief was right there. If I had just let the dam break, the headache would have vanished. The cortisol would have flushed. The peace would have returned, but I chose the pain of "strength" over the healing of "weakness."

PART V: THE COMMAND TO LAMENT

This brings us back to the command.

Why the Sackcloth? Why the ashes? Why did they do this?

They were not masochists. They were wise.

They understood that the mind can lie, but the body

keeps the score. They knew that you can not think your way out of a betrayal. You have to move your way out of it.

The Sackcloth was a **Somatic Intervention**.

Goat hair is itchy. It is uncomfortable. When you put it on, it creates a constant, low-level irritation on the skin.

Why is this helpful? Trauma makes us dissociate. When we are overwhelmed, we check out. We float away. We go numb.

The itch of the sackcloth forced you to stay in their body. It grounded them. It makes you present.

It prevented them from ignoring the pain. It forced them to face the toxic load head-on so they could process it and be done with it.

God's command to lament is a command to be honest.

When we refuse to lament, when we dry the tears too fast, when we rush to the victory lap, we are not being faithful.

The "Issue in the Tissue" is simply a prayer that got stuck. It is a lament that was denied its voice. We need to recover the Sackcloth.

I do not mean we need to buy goat hair shirts. I mean we need to recover the Time and the Permission to come apart.

We need to stop praising the "Strong Black Woman" for how much pain she can swallow, and start praising her for how much she can release. We need to stop telling our sons that tears equate weakness, and start teaching them that tears are the exhaust pipe for the engine of the heart.

We need to understand that the toxic load is the barrier to the presence of the Lord. You cannot be full of God if you are full of self, and you cannot be full of peace if you are full of poison.

In the next part of this book, we are going to look at the **Prescription**. We are going to look at the four specific tools God gave us to drain the poison and scrub the vessel clean.

We start with the House of Mourning.

Chapter 3: The Nervous System's War

We tend to think of weeping as a passive act, a moment of weakness where we dissolve into a puddle. We picture the crying person as limp, inactive, and defeated, but physiologically, this image is entirely wrong.

A full-blown episode of sobbing is an athletic event. It is a high-intensity interval workout for the respiratory, muscular, and vascular systems. It engages the diaphragm, the intercostal muscles of the ribs, the abdominals, the throat, the neck, and the face. It burns calories. It spikes heart rate variability. It alters blood pressure.

The act of suppressing a cry is war. It is a civil war fought within the confines of your own skin. It is a violent negotiation between two pilots trying to fly the plane of your body in opposite directions at the same time, and like any war, it leaves collateral damage.

In this chapter, we are going to look at the mechanics of this internal battle. We are going to examine why the "lump in your throat" hurts so much, why "holding it together" gives you a pounding headache, and why the peace of God, the Shalom we are all desperate for, is biologically impossible as long as we are fighting this war.

PART I: THE TWO PILOTS

To understand the war within, we have to look at the control panel. The human body is regulated by the **Autonomic Nervous System (ANS)**. This is the master computer that manages everything you don't have to think about: your heartbeat, your digestion, your breathing rate, and your pupil dilation.

The ANS is divided into two distinct branches. They

function like a seesaw. When one goes up, the other usually goes down.

1. The Sympathetic Nervous System (The Accelerator) This is the system of mobilization. It is responsible for the "Fight or Flight" response. When the brain perceives a threat, whether it's a predator in the bushes or a harsh word from a spouse, the sympathetic system slams on the gas.

The heart pumps faster to move blood to the muscles. The lungs dilate to take in more oxygen. The eye pupils dilate to sharpen vision. The digestion in the gut stops. The goal is to survive the threat by action.

2. The Parasympathetic Nervous System (The Brake) This is the system of restoration. It is responsible for the "Rest and Digest" or "Feed and Breed" response. When the threat has passed, the parasympathetic system pulls the brake.

The heart slows down. The muscles relax and become heavy. The digestion in the gut resumes. Saliva and tears are produced. The goal is to survive the peace by recovery.

Crying is **The Brake**. Dr. Ad Vingerhoets points out that while crying might start with high arousal (distress), the act of weeping is a parasympathetic function. It is the body's attempt to slam on the brakes. It is the mechanism designed to bring you down from the panic of the sympathetic spike back to the baseline of peace.

What happens when you refuse to let the brake engage? When your biology screams "Slow Down!" (Tears), but your will screams "Keep Going!" (Suppression) you get **The Nervous System's War**.

You are pressing the accelerator and the brake to the floorboard at the exact same time. The engine screams. The tires smoke. The frame shudders. You are creating massive amounts of heat and friction inside your own body. This friction is what I lived for the majority of my life.

PART II: THE STRATEGY OF PREEMPTIVE STRIKES

I mentioned earlier that I was a sensitive child. I felt everything. I remember clearly how much empathy I had. I recall a fishing trip with my uncle back in the 90s. He suffered from Crohn's Disease. In those days, the management of the disease was primitive, and he had a reaction to the medication that made him permanently slow.

We were out by the water, my uncle, my mom, my little

cousin, and me. I watched him struggle just to put the worm on the hook. His hands were shaking.

At one point, he had to leave to find a bathroom. When he came back, the trip was over. He had soiled himself.

I remember the silence of the car ride home. Mostly, I remember the crushing weight of sadness I felt for him. It was not pity. It was a deep, resonant ache. I questioned God that night. "Why does he have to live like that?"

That sensitivity extended to everyone. I saw people begging on the street. I was instantly bothered. I saw people broken, and I felt their cracks in my own bones.

There was a danger to this empathy, because I felt so deeply, I was easily wounded. Words cut me like knives. A sarcastic comment from a teacher, a jeer from a classmate, a disappointment from a parent did not just bounce off. They penetrated.

I knew that if I let the words land, I would cry, and tear equated weakness. The world swallows up the weak. I decided to intercept the words before they could land. I learned to react before I would get emotional.

If I even sensed a threat my counter-attack was to become quick-witted, defensive, or angry.

This is a classic biological maneuver. I was using the **Sympathetic Nervous System** (Rage/Fight) to override the **Parasympathetic Nervous System** (Grief/Tears).

Anger feels powerful. Sadness feels vulnerable. Anger pumps you up. Sadness brings you low. Anger pushes people away. Sadness draws them in.

I did not want to be drawn in. I wanted to be safe, so I used anger or comedy as a shield. I used toughness as a bunker.

I did not know it then, but I was engaging in **The Mutation of Shame**. I was taking the raw energy of hurt and chemically converting it into the kinetic energy of hostility. I was burning the fuel of my own soul to keep the walls up. It worked. People stopped messing with me. I stopped crying. I was somewhat able to mask my soft heart with the hard heart I prayed for.

PART III: THE ANATOMY OF THE LUMP

There is a specific physical sensation that every tearless person knows intimately. It is the **Globus Sensation**, or the lump in the throat. It feels like a golf ball is lodged in your esophagus. You swallow hard, trying to push it down, but it bounces right back up. It hurts. It feels tight, sharp, and suffocating. The lump in the throat is not a metaphor. It is a muscle war.

To understand the lump, you must understand the glottis. The glottis is the opening between your vocal cords in the larynx (voice box). It is the gateway to your lungs. It operates like a camera shutter, opening and closing to control airflow.

When your emotional brain (the Amygdala) registers deep sadness or distress, it signals the sympathetic nervous system. The body interprets this distress as a need for oxygen. You are about to sob.

A sob is a heavy, rhythmic gasping for air. To facilitate this, the brain tells the throat muscles to expand in order to open the glottis to prepare for a cry. The muscles of the throat pull the airway open to its maximum width.

BUT, your conscious will steps in. You are in public. Men don't cry.

To stop a cry, you have to perform the act of swallowing. You have to swallow the mucus and tears that are draining into the back of your throat. You have to literally swallow your pride.

The mechanics of swallowing require the exact opposite configuration. To swallow, the glottis must close tightly to prevent fluid from entering your lungs. If it did not close, you would choke or drown. Your conscious will tells you to close the glottis, so you swallow it down.

The tetanic contraction is the war. Your autonomic brain is pulling the muscles open. Your conscious will is pulling the muscles closed. They are pulling in opposite directions at full strength, simultaneously.

The lump you feel is sheer muscle strain. It is the feeling of your own anatomy tearing itself apart. It is the tension of the dam holding back the river.

This is why, the moment you finally let go and start to sob, the lump instantly disappears. When you surrender to the cry, the conscious will stops fighting. The swallowing reflex yields. The glottis opens to allow the heavy, rhythmic gasping of the sob, and the tension resolves.

The lump is not the sadness. The lump is the resistance to sadness.

God designed the throat to open during grief, to let the wail out. When we force it closed, we are literally strangling our own expression. We are choking on our own silence.

PART IV: THE HEADACHE OF RESISTANCE

One of the most common complaints of people who hold it in is a specific type of headache. It is not a migraine, and it is not quite a tension headache. It is a pounding, throbbing pressure behind the eyes and at the base of the skull. It adds insult to injury. Not only are you heartbroken, but now your head feels like it is in a vise. This pain is the receipt for the energy you just spent fighting God's design.

The Vascular Throb occurs when the body prepares to cry, the tear ducts (lacrimal glands) need a massive supply of blood and fluid. The blood vessels in the face and head dilate (widen) to deliver this payload.

At the same time, the sinuses swell. The liquid language is getting ready to flow through the eyes and the nose.

When you suppress the cry, you do not stop the blood flow. You just stop the release. The vessels remain dilated. The blood is pounding through the temples, bringing high pressure to the sensitive meninges (the covering of the brain).

Simultaneously, you are engaging the muscles of the face to hide the emotion. This is the muscular mask. The frontalis (forehead) pulls up to look alert. The corrugator (brow) crunches down to look serious. The orbicularis oculi (eye muscles) squint tight to keep the water in. The masseter (jaw) clenches to stop the lip from quivering.

You are creating a rigid mask of tension. You are isometric-holding your face in a neutral expression against the force of a screaming emotion. Sustaining this tension for minutes or hours creates a buildup of lactic acid in the facial muscles. This refers pain directly into the skull. The headache is the physical manifestation of the mental effort it takes to be "strong."

This is the irony of our "strength." We think we are preserving our energy by not crying. We think crying is draining, but science proves the opposite. Suppression burns more calories than release. Holding the beach ball underwater takes constant, exhausting effort. Letting it pop to the surface takes one moment of release, and then... rest.

PART V: THE PEACE WE LOST

Why does this matter spiritually? Why is a book about God talking about glottis muscles and vascular dilation?

Because peace (Shalom) is a physiological state.

We often treat peace as a spiritual idea, like a mystical vibe that descends on us during a worship song. In the Bible, peace is wholeness. It is the absence of chaos. It is the restoration of order. It is His Presence that is your peace.

You can not have Peace in your spirit if you have a War in your nervous system.

If your sympathetic and parasympathetic systems are locked in a cage match, one is trying to scream, and the other trying to strangle the scream, you are in a state of internal violence.

You might be smiling. You might be saying, "I'm blessed." You might be lifting your hands in church, but when you are in constant emotional suppression you have no peace. When you are in the headache stage, you are in a ceasefire, and ceasefires are fragile.

This is why so many believers are one bad day away from a meltdown. They are walking around with a system operating at 99% capacity. They have no margin.

God wants to give us peace, but He cannot give peace to a system that refuses to surrender.

This brings us back to the sackcloth. The sackcloth was the ancient technology for ending the war. When the biblical times men put on the goat hair and covered themselves in ashes, they were declaring a winner in the internal battle. He was saying grief wins.

He stopped trying to swallow the lump. He opened his throat and wailed. He stopped trying to hide the tears. He let them flow into the dust. He stopped trying to look strong. He covered himself in ashes. In that surrender, the war ended. The glottis opened. The pressure released. The headache faded. The cortisol flushed out. Then,and only then, was there room for His Presence to enter.

You can not be full of the Holy Spirit if you are full of yourself. Holding it together is the ultimate act of self. It is self-protection. It is self-preservation. It is self-image.

Lament is the death of self. It is the admission that "I cannot handle this." It is the moment we stop trying to be the captains of our own souls and let the ship go down, and it is there, in the wreckage of our composure, that His Presence meets us.

PART VI: THE INVITATION TO LOSE

I spent my entire life trying to win the war. I tried to beat my sensitivity into submission. I tried to outsmart my own biology. I failed. All I got was a hard heart and a tired body.

The invitation of this book, and the invitation of our Father is to lose the war. It is an invitation to stop fighting the lump in your throat. To stop managing your image. To stop fearing the liquid language.

We are the crying babies. We are the ones who break. God is the Father who can translate your tears into words, and those tears into victory.

He is not asking for our strength. He is asking for our honesty. He knows that the only way to get the "Issues out of the Tissues" is to open the valve.

Chapter 4:

The King Who Cried (David vs. Cain)

You are in the middle of a heated argument. You are furious. You feel a righteous fire in your belly, and you are ready to verbally dismantle your opponent. You have your arguments lined up like soldiers. You want to yell. You want to pound the table. You want to look formidable.

Instead, a traitorous sensation begins in your face. Your chin begins to quiver. The muscles of your throat constrict into a painful knot. Burning tears of rage commence.

It is a moment of profound humiliation. You are trying to project power, but your face is projecting surrender. You try to force it down, demanding that your body get back in line, but the resistance only makes the sobs more violent. You feel betrayed by your own biology. You are furious, but you look broken.

This specific type of crying feels physiologically distinct from the heavy, slow tears of grief. Grief tears feel like a release, while rage tears feel like a burn. They come with a distinct sensation of heat in the skin and a pounding, vascular headache that arrives almost instantly.

The reason for this agony is cognitive dissonance. In this moment, your body is effectively at war with itself.

PART I: THE PHYSIOLOGY OF THE GLITCH

To understand the pain of the rage tear, we must look at the collision of the nervous systems.

When you are enraged, your **Sympathetic Nervous System** (the accelerator) is fully engaged. It is pumping adrenaline and cortisol to prepare you for a fight. Your muscles are tense, ready to strike or defend. Your blood pressure is sky-high.

Mentally and physically, you are in a high-power position. You are a predator ready to pounce.

For some reason a sense of powerlessness, frustration, or blocked action, and your brain triggers the crying reflex.

As we have learned, crying is a **Parasympathetic** (the brake) function. It is a low-power, submissive biological response designed to signal surrender and induce calm.

So, you have a physiological paradox. One system is shouting "Attack!" and the other system is shouting "Yield!" simultaneously.

You are pressing the accelerator and the brake at the same time. The heat you feel is the friction of these two systems grinding against each other. The exhaustion that follows a bout of angry crying is profound because you have not just released emotion. You have endured a massive internal short-circuit.

Psychologists suggest that rage tears are almost always linked to a feeling of impotence.

We rarely cry when we are winning a fight. If you can punch the enemy, or if you can verbally dominate the argument, the energy is discharged through the action. The steam escapes through the whistle.

Rage tears happen when we are frustrated. The literal definition of frustrated means "to be blocked." The energy of the anger builds up, but there is nowhere for it to go. You cannot hit your boss. You cannot scream at the police officer. You cannot force your spouse to understand you. The kinetic energy hits a wall and ricochets back inward.

The tear is the body's emergency safety valve. It says, "If I don't vent this pressure, the machine will break."

As frustrating and embarrassing as they are, these tears are a mercy. They are the mechanism that prevents the vessel from exploding.

PART II: THE HYDRAULIC THEORY OF AGGRESSION

If you talk to prison psychiatrists, experts in criminology, or domestic violence counselors, they will tell you a chilling truth. The men who commit the most violent acts are often the men who can not weep.

This concept is grounded in what psychology calls the **Hydraulic Model of Aggression**.

Imagine the human emotional system as a steam engine.

Life generates heat. Trauma, grief, shame, betrayal, and rejection boil the water of the soul, creating pressure (steam). In a healthy system, the steam escapes through the whistle (verbal communication: "I am hurt") or the release valve (tears: physical processing). If a person has been conditioned to believe that crying is weak they suppress the valve. They hold it in.

The laws of physics apply to the soul as much as they do to the engine. *Energy cannot be destroyed and it can only be transferred.*

If the pressure can not escape as through tears, it transforms into kinetic energy. Violence. The steam does not vanish. It blows the boiler apart.

This is why we see a direct correlation between **Alexithymia** and violent behavior.

Alexithymia is a personality trait characterized by the inability to identify and describe emotions in the self. It literally means "no words for emotions." A person with high alexithymia feels the physical sensation of distress, but they cannot connect it to an emotion like sadness or grief. They only register it as a threat. They cannot process the sadness verbally or through tears, they are forced to process it physically. They punch a wall. They break a window. They hurt a partner.

The violence is not a sign of toughness. It is a sign of a broken drainage system. It is the explosion of a tank that was never allowed to vent.

PART III: THE MUTATION OF SHAME

Dr. James Gilligan is a psychiatrist who spent decades directing the Center for the Study of Violence at Harvard Medical School. He spent his career sitting in cells with murderers, gang leaders, and violent offenders, asking a single question: "Why?"

He sought the "pathogen" that causes violence. Was it poverty? Was it genetics? Was it drugs?

His conclusion was singular. While those factors play a role, the root cause of all violence, Gilligan argued, is shame. Specifically, it is unacknowledged shame.

Here is the pathway of the mutation:

The Injury: A man feels disrespected, rejected, or heartbroken. His wife leaves him, or he loses his job, or he is humiliated in front of his peers.

The Natural Response: His biology wants to grieve. It

wants to cry. This is the healthy, homeostatic response to hurt.

The Block: His cultural conditioning tells him that crying is "feminine," "soft," or "weak." To cry is to admit defeat. To cry is to be vulnerable. To a man whose ego is already fragile, the idea of crying induces more shame.

The Mutation: To protect the ego from the unbearable feeling of "weakness" (sadness), the brain instantly converts the energy into "strength" (rage).

This conversion happens in a split second. Sadness feels vulnerable. It collapses the chest. It lowers the head. While anger feels powerful, it puffs out the chest. It raises the chin.

The brain makes a lightning-fast switch to save the self. He replaces the tears with the fist. Violence, then, is simply grief turned inside out. It is sadness that has been armored.

When you see a man in a rage, screaming at a cashier or punching a steering wheel, you are not looking at a powerful man. You are looking at a man who is terrified of his own grief. He is performing anger because he does not have the courage to perform sadness.

PART IV: THE "LOADED GUN" PHYSIOLOGY

The physiological cost of being a tearless man is that you live in a permanent state of adrenaline toxicity.

As we discussed in Chapter 1, emotional tears remove ACTH and trigger the parasympathetic nervous system to calm the body down. They are the reset button.

When a person does hit that button, and they experience trauma but do not cry, those stress chemicals (adrenaline, cortisol, norepinephrine) remain circulating in the bloodstream. The body stays in a state of **Chronic Hyper-Arousal**.

They experience muscle tension. Their jaws are perpetually tight. Their shoulders are raised. Their hands are often clenched.

They experience cardiovascular stress. Their resting heart rate is elevated. Their blood pressure is high.

They experience cognitive tunneling. Their brain remains in "threat detection" mode, scanning their environment for insults or dangers.

This is the loaded gun state. For a healthy person who cries and processes emotion, a minor annoyance, like someone cutting them off in traffic, is irritating, but manageable. Their baseline stress is low, so they have room to absorb the shock.

For the tearless man, his baseline stress is already at 90%. He is vibrating with ten years of unwept tears and unresolved traumas. He has no buffer.

So, when the car cuts him off, it is not just a traffic violation. It is the spark that lands in the powder keg. He explodes in disproportionate road rage. He screams, he chases the other car, he pulls a weapon.

To the observer, it looks like insanity. "Why is he so angry about a lane change?" He is not angry about the lane change. He is angry about his father. He is angry about his divorce. He is angry about his shame. The traffic incident was just the permission slip his body was waiting for to release the pressure he has been carrying for a decade.

He is chemically walking around with a loaded gun, waiting for the world to pull the trigger.

PART V: BIBLICAL ARCHETYPES: CAIN VS. DAVID

The Bible does not shy away from this psychology. In fact, it offers us a stark, bloody archetype of the tearless man in the very first generation of humanity after the Fall.

Consider the story of Cain in Genesis 4. Cain brings an offering to the Lord from the fruit of the ground. God looks with favor on Abel's offering, but not on Cain's. Cain experiences a profound rejection. He feels shame. He feels less than his brother.

Watch the diagnosis God gives him in verse 6: *"Why are you angry? Why is your face downcast?"*

The Hebrew word for "downcast" here implies depression, a falling of the countenance. Cain is sad. He is hurt. He is grieving the loss of God's approval.

Notice Cain does not weep. He does not fall on his face. He does not lament. He says nothing. He bottles the rejection. The sadness mutates.

God warns him explicitly: *"If you do not do what is right, sin is crouching at your door; it desires to have you, but you must rule over it."*

God is warning him about the mutation. He is saying, "Cain, you are standing at a crossroads. You can process this pain, or you can let it devour you."

Cain chooses the path of the tearless. He invites his brother into the field. There, the pent-up energy of rejection explodes into the kinetic energy of murder. He kills the source of his shame.

The suppression of grief led to the shedding of blood.

Now, contrast this with **David**, the King of Israel.

David was a man of blood. He was a warrior who killed the giant, Goliath, and commanded armies. He killed a lion. He killed a bear. By no means would anybody consider him a weak man.

Yet, David is the Bible's most prolific weeper. When he loses his best friend Jonathan, he weeps. When he loses his infant son, he weeps. When he is betrayed by his son Absalom, he weeps as he climbs the Mount of Olives, his head covered and his feet bare. In Psalm 6:6, he writes: *"I am worn out from my groaning. All night long I flood my bed with weeping and drench my couch with tears."*

David had a release valve. He knew the language of Lament.

Despite his sins,including adultery and murder, David never became a sociopath. He never became hard-hearted. When the prophet Nathan confronted him about his sin with

Bathsheba, David did not lash out in rage. He did not kill the messenger to protect his ego.

David broke. He wrote Psalm 51. He wept. David knew how to release his pain to God, his heart remained flesh rather than turning to stone. He processed his trauma rather than projecting it onto others.

Cain became a wanderer, hardened and isolated, marked by his violence. David became a man after God's own heart. The difference was not the severity of their trauma because both men faced rejection and betrayal. The difference was the liquidity of their response.

PART VI: THE GENERATIONAL CURSE OF THE DRY EYE

This pattern does not just affect individuals, it shapes families and cultures.

We often talk about generational curses in spiritual terms, but there is a biological mechanism to them. The curse is often the inherited inability to lament.

Imagine a father who was taught that "men don't cry." He suppresses his grief, his trauma, and his fear. He cannot process these emotions, they mutate into irritability and rage. He becomes a "volcanic" father, emotionally distant most of the time, but prone to sudden explosions of anger.

His son watches this. The son learns two lessons. Dad is scary when he is mad. Dad never cries, so crying must be for the weak.

The son grows up terrified of his own sadness. He learns to stuff his own pain to avoid being weak like the victims his father despised. He adopts the same "loaded gun" physiology.

Fast forward twenty years. The son is now a father. He hits a moment of stress. He does not have the tools to cry, so he screams. The cycle repeats.

This is how trauma travels through bloodlines. It travels on the back of silence. It travels because the father refuses to use the release valve, so the son inherits the explosion.

To break a generational curse often requires a man to do the one thing his father never did. Weep.

When a father cries in front of his son it is not out of weakness, but out of honest, processed grief, and he is breaking the cycle. He is showing his son that it is safe to be sad. You do not have to turn this into a fist. You can turn it into water.

PART VII: THE IMPRECATORY TEARS: A HOLY RAGE

The Bible contains **Imprecatory Psalms**. Prayers of intense anger. Psalm 58 prays for the teeth of the wicked to be broken. Psalm 137 prays for violence against the oppressors. Notice the context. These are prayers.

The Psalmist is not going out and breaking teeth. He is not killing Babylonians. He is bringing his rage to God in the form of a lament.

This is the crucial distinction. Violence is taking rage out on your neighbor. Lament is taking rage out on God. God is big enough to handle our rage. Our neighbor is not.

When we cry tears of rage in prayer, when we sob over the injustice of the world, when we scream at the heavens because of abuse or cancer or corruption, we are doing something holy. We are giving the energy back to the only One who can handle it righteously.

These imprecatory prayers are safe. They allow us to honor the anger without sinning by hurting someone else. As Ephesians 4:26 says, *"Be angry and do not sin."* The space between "Be angry" and "do not sin" is often filled with tears. If you skip the tears, the anger almost always becomes sin.

PART VIII: CONCLUSION: LIQUID VS. SOLID

There is a sombre poetic truth here that every society, every father, and every individual should heed. **If you do not shed water, you will eventually shed blood.**

Water (or tears) is fluid. It cleanses. It flows. It yields. It creates a soft heart.

Blood (or violence) is the result of a hard, brittle structure shattering under pressure. It stains. It takes life.

The tearless person is not actually stronger, they are much more dangerous. They are brittle. A piece of iron is strong, but it cannot bend, but under enough pressure, it snaps. A willow branch is soft, but it bends in the storm and survives.

By denying the biological reset mechanism of crying, the tearless man forces his body to store the trauma. Violence, scientifically speaking, is often just the externalization of internal pain that was never allowed to wash away.

We have a choice in how we handle the pressure of living in a broken world. We can operate the machine as God designed it, using the valve of the tear to release the steam, or we can weld the valve shut, look tough for a season, and wait for the inevitable explosion.

What happens when the trauma is not a sudden event that makes us angry, but a slow, grinding reality that we try to forget? What happens when the mind tries to move on, but the body refuses? This brings us to the science of **somatic memory**, and the strange reality that our tissues hold onto our history long after our brains have let it go.

Chapter 5:

The House of Mourning (Lament)

PART I: THE UNWANTED HOUSE

If you were to create a map of the human heart, there are certain neighborhoods we all want to live in. We want to live in the House of Mirth. We want to live in the House of Success. We want to live in the House of Certainty.

There is one house on the block that we avoid at all costs. The windows are dark. The air is heavy. The music is somber. We drive past it with our eyes fixed on the road, terrified that if we stop, we might get stuck there. This is the **House of Mourning**.

We view this house as a failure. In our modern culture of "Good Vibes Only," sadness is treated like a contagious disease. If you are sad for too long, people start to worry. They offer you platitudes. They say, "Everything happens for a reason," or "At least you have your health," or "God works all things for good." They try to rush you out the door. Tears make people uncomfortable.

We run from sorrow like it is a burning building. We avoid grief like the plague.

But the Bible says something shocking about this house. In **Ecclesiastes 7**, King Solomon—the wisest man who ever lived, drops a nugget:

> *It is better to go to a house of mourning than to go to a house of feasting, for death is the destiny of everyone; the living should take this to heart. Frustration is better than laughter, because a sad face is good for the heart.* ***The heart of the wise is in the house of mourning, but the heart of fools is in the house of pleasure.***

-Ecclesiastes 7:2-4

Solomon is arguing that wisdom is not found in the party. It is not found in the promotion. It is not found in the victory lap. Wisdom is found in the funeral home. Wisdom is found in the hospital waiting room. Wisdom is found in the wreckage.

Why?

The House of Mourning is the only place where the illusions of life are stripped away. In the House of Feasting, we can pretend that we are in control. We can pretend that we are immortal. We can distract ourselves with noise, wine, and applause.

In the House of Mourning, the noise stops. We are forced to confront the reality of our fragility. We are forced to admit that we are not God, and this admission is a terrifying, beautiful surrender that is the beginning of **His Presence**.

This is why Lament is the first pillar of our prescription. Lament is not wallowing. It is not "feeling sorry for yourself." Lament is the deliberate decision to enter the House of Mourning and sit there until the work is done. It is the spiritual discipline of clearing the debris so that His Spirit can enter.

PART II: THE ARCHITECTURE OF THE SCREAM

How do we do it?

Most of us have no idea how to lament because we have never been taught. We know how to complain, which is toxic. We know how to repress, which is toxic. Yet, we do not know how to lament, which is healing.

The Book of Psalms serves as our manual. Out of the 150 Psalms, roughly one-third, over sixty of them, are Psalms of Lament. They are songs of disorientation, anger, and fear.

They follow a specific architectural structure. It is a curve. It is a journey that moves the soul from the pit of biological panic to the peak of spiritual peace. Let us learn to walk this curve.

Stage 1: The Scream (The Question)

Every true lament begins with a scream.

It starts with the **Protest**. It starts with the unfiltered, raw data of the nervous system being dumped onto the table.

Look at **Psalm 13**:

> *How long, Lord? Will you forget me forever? How long will you hide your face from me? How long*

must I wrestle with my thoughts and day after day have sorrow in my heart? How long will my enemy triumph over me?

-Psalm 13:1-2

Four times in two verses, David screams, "How long?"

This is the language of the sympathetic nervous system. This is the Amygdala hijacking the brain. David is not being polite. He is not filtering his theology. He is accusing God of amnesia "Will you forget me?" and negligence "Will you hide your face?"

This stage is crucial. We often try to skip it because it feels disrespectful. We think we can not question God. "Who are we to question God?"

If you don't start with the scream, you are starting with a lie. If you are angry, but you pray, "Lord, I just want to thank you for this day," you are lying. You cannot build a relationship on a lie. God wants the truth, even if the truth is ugly.

The Scream is the opening of the release valve. It is the moment the liquid language begins to flow. It is the removal of the mask.

Stage 2: The Silence (The Sackcloth)

After the scream comes the **Sit**.

In Biblical time tradition, after tearing the clothes and wailing, the mourner would sit in the ashes. They would become still.

> *I am worn out from my groaning. All night long I flood my bed with weeping and drench my couch with tears.*
>
> ***-Psalm 6:6***

This is the stage of **Grounding**.

When we are in high-stress trauma, our brains want to dissociate. We want to float away. We want to numb out with Netflix, food, or work. We find comfort in distractions.

The Sackcloth stage forces us to stay in the room. It forces us to feel the itch of reality. It forces us to dwell in the sadness.

This is the hardest part for the modern believer. We are addicted to instant gratification. We want the grief to be over in a weekend, but the soul moves at the speed of agriculture. It takes time.

In this silence, the manganese is leaving the brain. The "issues in the tissues" are being processed. The body is doing the heavy lifting of metabolizing the pain.

Stage 3: The Shift (The Pivot)

Then, something miraculous happens. If you stay in the House of Mourning long enough the atmosphere changes. There is a moment in almost every Lament Psalm where the tone snaps. It pivots.

> *But I trust in your unfailing love; my heart rejoices in your salvation.*
>
> ***-Psalm 13:5***

This is the **Shift**. The Hebrew word often used here is a small particle called the *Waw Adversative*. In English, it is the word **"**But" or "Yet."

"My life is falling apart... **BUT** I trust in you."

"I am surrounded by enemies... **YET** you are a shield around me."

This shift is not forced. It is not the result of positive thinking. It is the biological and spiritual result of the release. The word "but" negates the previous statement. In that moment you realize "you are protected" and "your life is not falling apart."

The pressure has been vented (Stage 1) and processed (Stage 2), the brain is no longer in panic. The fog clears. The liquid language has done its work. The static is gone. The lines are clear.

Stage 4: The Song (The Earned Praise)

The final stage is the song.

> *I will sing the Lord's praise, for he has been good to me.*
>
> ***-Psalm 13:6***

This is the return of the Presence. All Laments end in **JOY**.

Your circumstances have not changed. In Psalm 13, the "enemy" is still there. The problem was not solved, but David was solved.

The song he sings in Verse 6 is different from the song he would have sung in Verse 1. It is deeper. It is darker. It is richer. It is a song that has been through the fire. This is **Earned Praise**.

Cheap praise is singing "God is good" when everything is going right. Earned praise is singing "God is good" when everything is going wrong, because you have wrestled with Him in the dark and found Him faithful.

PART III: THE TANGENT OF ECCLESIASTES

Let's go back to Solomon's strange advice in Ecclesiastes

7. Why is the heart of the wise in the House of Mourning?

Solomon creates a contrast between two types of laughter:

> *Like the crackling of thorns under the pot, so is the laughter of fools. This too is meaningless.*
>
> ***-Ecclesiastes 7:6***

Have you ever thrown thorns or dry twigs into a fire? They flare up instantly. They make a loud pop and crackle. They are bright and hot for about three seconds. And then... ash.

Solomon says this is the joy of the world. It is the joy of the "House of Feasting." It is the dopamine hit of the new car, the viral post, the party or the sugar. It is loud, it is bright, and it burns out instantly, leaving you colder than before.

The House of Mourning produces a different kind of heat. It produces the heat of coals. Coals take a long time to light. They do not crackle. They do not flare. They burn for hours. They provide sustained warmth through the long night.

Lament turns our hearts into coals. It strips away superficial happiness and ignites the deep, slow-burning fuel of joy. Joy is not the absence of pain. Joy is the presence of God within the pain.

When we run from the House of Mourning, we are choosing the cheap, fast dopamine over the deep, slow oxytocin of the Spirit. We are choosing to be entertained rather than sustained.

PART IV: THE COMMAND TO LAMENT

We need to stop viewing Lament as a lack of faith. We need to stop viewing tears as a failure.

When Jesus says, *"Blessed are those who mourn, for they will be comforted,"* He is giving us a biological equation. No mourning equals no comfort. No sackcloth equals no peace. If you skip the mourning, you skip the comfort. You skip the Presence.

God is inviting us into the House of Mourning not to punish us, but to heal us. He knows that the only way to get the toxic load out of our bodies is to let the liquid flow.

The wisdom is in the mourning because the truth is in the mourning, and once we have cleared the debris we are ready for the next step. We are ready to sharpen our focus. We are ready to tune the receiver.

We are ready for the **Empty Stomach.**

Chapter 6:

The Empty Stomach (Fasting)

PART I: THE SIN OF THE BUFFET

If I asked you to name the sin of Sodom and Gomorrah, what would you say?

Most of us would immediately point to sexual immorality. We would talk about lust, perversion, and violence. The name Sodom itself has become linguistically synonymous with sexual deviance.

The prophet Ezekiel gives a different diagnosis. In **Eze-**

kiel 16:49, God pulls back the curtain on the root cause of that city's destruction, and the list of charges is terrifyingly familiar to the modern Western believer:

> *Now this was the sin of your sister Sodom: She and her daughters were arrogant,* ***overfed and unconcerned****; they did not help the poor and needy.*
>
> ***-Ezekiel 16:49***

Arrogant. Overfed. Unconcerned.

The Hebrew word for overfed implies a surfeit of food, a state of constant satiety. They were a people who never knew hunger. They moved from one meal to the next, one pleasure to the next, one comfort to the next. This physical fullness led directly to the third charge of being unconcerned.

The Hebrew word here is *shaqat*, meaning "undisturbed," "quiet," or "at ease." It implies numbness. They were so stuffed with food and comfort that they could no longer feel the pain of the poor, the urgency of justice, or the voice of God. They were numbed by their own fullness.

This is the spiritual danger of the buffet. It is the danger of the pantry that is always full and the refrigerator that is never empty.

We tend to view Fasting as a radical, extreme practice reserved for monks and fanatics. We view eating as the neutral baseline, but biologically and spiritually, the state of being constantly overfed is not neutral. It is a sedative.

When the stomach is full, the spirit is often asleep. This is why fasting is the second pillar of our prescription. It is the antidote to the Sodomite spirit. It is the deliberate embrace of the fasting to break the spell of comfort and wake up the soul.

PART II: THE PHYSIOLOGY OF THE SLUMBER

To understand why fasting wakes us up, we have to understand why eating puts us to sleep. The human body is an energy management system. Every task requires blood flow, oxygen, and glucose.

Digestion is one of the most energy-expensive tasks the human body performs. When you eat a large meal your autonomic nervous system initiates a massive reallocation of resources. It triggers **Splanchnic Circulation**.

The body shunts a significant percentage of your total

blood volume away from your muscles and your brain and directs it to the stomach and intestines. It takes energy to break down steak, process sugar, and extract nutrients.

While this is happening, the brain enters a state of low-energy maintenance. You know this feeling. It is "Food Coma" or "The Itis." You feel lethargic. You feel heavy. Your thinking becomes slower. Your focus blurs. You just want to sit on the couch and zone out.

This is a biological necessity. You can not hunt a lion and digest a gazelle at the same time. Spiritually, this creates a problem. If we are constantly eating, grazing from breakfast to snack to lunch to dinner to midnight snack, our bodies are perpetually stuck in digest mode. Our blood is always in our gut, not in our brain.We are biologically dulled.

This dullness creates a "static" on the spiritual line. It is hard to hear the whisper of the Holy Spirit when your body is shouting for a nap. It is hard to have spiritual hunger when you have zero physical hunger. Fasting flips the switch.

PART III: THE HUNTER'S MIND (THE SCIENCE OF GHRELIN)

When you stop eating for 12, 18, or 24 hours, the body undergoes a radical physiological shift. As the stomach empties, it secretes a hormone called **Ghrelin**.

We usually think of Ghrelin as the bad guy. It is the hunger hormone. It is the chemical that makes your stomach growl and tells your brain to eat.

Neuroscientists have discovered that Ghrelin does something profound. Ghrelin crosses the blood-brain barrier and acts directly on the hippocampus, the region of the brain responsible for memory, learning, and spatial navigation.

Ghrelin enhances cognitive function. To the evolutionist, this makes perfect sense. If an animal is hungry, it needs to remember where the food sources are. It needs to be alert, sharp, and focused to hunt. A hungry wolf is a focused wolf. A full wolf is a sleepy wolf.

When you fast, you are flooding your brain with Ghrelin. You are chemically hacking your mind into a state of heightened seeking. You are entering hunter mode.

In a spiritual context, we are co-opting this biological mechanism. We are taking the body's urge to find food and sublimating it into an urge to find God.

The clarity that comes after 18 hours of fasting is not an illusion. It is a survival mechanism. The brain is dialed in. The fog lifts. The static clears. You have ADHD. You are hyperfocused.

This is why Jesus fasted for 40 days before launching His ministry. He was not just proving a point. He was preparing His vessel. He was engaging the hunter's mind to battle with Satan. He needed maximum spiritual and mental acuity, and He knew that a full stomach would be a liability and a distraction

Fasting provides extreme focus. It cleans the receiver so that the signal from Heaven comes through in High Definition.

PART IV: THE TWELVE-HOUR WINDOW

This brings us to a practical point that the modern church often tries to dodge. What counts as a fast? We have become experts at the partial fast. We give up chocolate. We give up social media. We give up meat.

While there is value in self-denial of any kind, biblically speaking, a fast involves the stomach, and it involves time.

If we look at the patterns in Scripture, there is a consistent rhythm. The Jewish day began at sundown. A standard fast was often from sun up to sun down or sundown to sundown.

Take **Judges 20:26**:

> *Then all the Israelites, the whole army, went up and came to Bethel, and they sat there before the Lord and wept. They fasted that day* ***until evening****...*

Or **2 Samuel 1:12**, when David and his men mourn for Saul:

> *They mourned and wept and fasted* ***till evening*** *for Saul and his son Jonathan...*

The biblical model suggests a minimum threshold. You can not fast for two hours between lunch and a late dinner. The biology requires a window of at least 12 hours to truly shift the body out of digest mode and into repair mode (Ketosis/Autophagy).

We find every excuse why we can not fast. "I have a condition that requires me to eat." or "I have to take medication that requires me to eat." The bottom line is Americans are overfed. A recent study published in *The Lancet* suggest 75% of American adults are overweight or obese. There is no reason we cannot fast for 12 hours. We sleep for 8 hours. That leaves only 4 hours of awake time to abstain.

God is not asking for the impossible. He is asking for the physiological shift. He is asking us to enter the zone where Ghrelin spikes and the mind clears. He is asking us to feel the emptiness so we can remember who fills us.

PART V: THE DANIEL FAST OR DIET

Every January, thousands of churches embark on the Daniel Fast for 21 days. We cut out meat, sugar, and wine, and we eat vegetables, legumes, and water. We treat this as a spiritual superpower.

In **Daniel 1**, Daniel refuses the King's food of meat and wine not specifically as a fast, but to avoid defiling himself with food sacrificed to idols. He chooses vegetables and water. As a result, he was healthier and stronger than the other young men.

My father did this. He went on the Daniel Fast for spiritual reasons. He has high blood pressure, high cholesterol, the standard toxic load issues we discussed in Chapter 2. Near the end of the fast, he went for his annual physical. The doctor looked at his blood work and said, "Whatever you are eating, keep it up. Your numbers are great."

It proves that eating clean honors the temple. It proves that vegetables are better for your arteries than fried chicken, but a diet is not a fast.

The Daniel Fast as we practice it is simply a healthier way of life. It is good stewardship, but it does not necessarily produce the empty stomach focus that is essential in this process. You can still be overfed on hummus and avocados. You can still be in a food coma from too many lentils.

If we want to see where Daniel truly fasted, we have to turn to **Daniel 9 and 10**.

In Daniel 9:3, Daniel writes: *"So I turned to the Lord God and pleaded with him in prayer and petition, in* ***fasting, and in sackcloth and ashes****."*

This was not a diet plan for better cholesterol. This was mourning. This was sackcloth. This was the denial of pleasure to access the Presence of the Lord.

He did not do it to get healthy. He did it to get a vision, and in verse 5, the vision comes. A man dressed in linen appears to him.

The diet in Daniel 1 gave him a healthy body. The fast in Daniel 10 gave him a spiritual breakthrough. We need both, but we must stop confusing the two.

PART VI: THE TRANSACTIONAL HERESY

Many believers view fasting as a transaction. I have a problem, so I will starve myself for three days. Then, God will bless me for my obedience.

This is simply a hunger strike. It is an attempt to manipulate God. It is treating God like a vending machine. If I put in enough "hunger coins," the blessing will drop out.

In **Isaiah 58**, the people of Israel are fasting, but God is not answering. They complain:

> *Why have we fasted," they say, "and you have not seen it? Why have we humbled ourselves, and you have not noticed?*
>
> ***- Isaiah 58:3***

God answers them with a stinging rebuke. He tells

them that their fasting is useless because their hearts are unchanged. They are fasting for personal gain while exploiting their workers. They are bowing their heads "like a reed" but ignoring the poor.

> *Is this not the fast that I have chosen: To loose the bonds of wickedness, to undo the heavy burdens, to let the oppressed go free, and that you break every yoke?*
>
> ***-Isaiah 58:6***

God is saying that fasting is not about changing His mind. It is about changing your heart.

Fasting is designed to break the yoke of the flesh. It is designed to break the tyranny of our own appetites. It is designed to make us soft to the needs of others (which connects to Giving in Chapter 7).

> *Now this was the sin of your sister Sodom: She and her daughters were arrogant,* ***overfed*** *and unconcerned;* ***they did not help the poor and needy.****"*
>
> ***-Ezekiel 16:49***

We do not fast to get God to do what *we* want. We fast to align ourselves with what He wants. We fast to tune the radio to His frequency, not to force Him to broadcast on ours.

PART VII: THE SECRET REWARD (MATTHEW 6)

This brings us to the instruction of Jesus in **Matthew 6**.

> *When you fast, do not look somber as the hypocrites do, for they disfigure their faces to show others they are fasting. Truly I tell you, they have received their reward in full.*
>
> ***-Matthew 6:16***

The Pharisees fasted for notoriety. They wanted the reward of the crowd. They wanted that pat on their back.

And Jesus says:

> *They got it. That's their reward. The applause of men.*
>
> ***-Matthew 6:2***

But then He offers a better reward:

> *But when you fast, put oil on your head and wash your face... and your Father, who sees what is*

done in secret, will reward you.

-Matthew 6:17-18

The reward of the secret place is being in His Presence. The reward is the restoration of the connection that was lost in Eden. The reward is a mind that is sharp enough to hear God's voice. The reward is a heart that is free from the addiction to comfort. The reward is peace.

PART VIII: THE COMMAND TO FOCUS

God commands us to fast because He knows we are addicted to the buffet of Sodom. He knows we are "overfed and unconcerned." He knows that our constant consumption is lulling us into a spiritual coma. He is not trying to starve us, He is trying to sharpen us.

When we fast, we are engaging a biological mechanism (Ghrelin/Focus) to achieve a spiritual end (Communion). We are telling our bodies, *"Man shall not live by bread alone."*

We are proving to our nervous systems that God is a better source of dopamine than a donut. Once the stomach is empty, and the mind is clear, and the debris of lament has been cleared away, we are finally ready to do the thing that is most contrary to our survival instinct.

We are ready to open our hands. We are ready for the biology of Giving.

Chapter 7:

The Open Hand (Giving)

PART I: THE LAW OF THE JUNGLE

If you watch a nature documentary long enough, you will eventually see the moment of the kill. A lioness takes down a gazelle. It is a moment of violent triumph, the culmination of patience, speed, and caloric expenditure. After the kill the lioness does not relax. She instantly transitions into a posture of extreme defense. She crouches over the carcass, ears flattened, teeth bared, scanning the horizon for hyenas or rival lions. She protects her kill.

This is the law of the jungle. It is the survival of the fittest in its purest form. In the wild, resources are scarce, and energy is expensive. You do not expend calories to hunt just to give the prize away. You hunt to eat. You hunt to survive. To keep what you catch is the primary directive of biological existence.

Human beings, despite our suits and our skyscrapers, still possess this animalistic hardware. We are hardwired for acquisition. When we earn a paycheck, when we close a deal, when we buy a house, our brains release dopamine.

This instinct creates a life lived entirely on defense. We build fences. We buy insurance. We pad our savings accounts. We hoard our time. We view the world as a zero-sum game where every resource given away is a resource lost. We walk through life with a posture of guarding, always watching the horizon for the hyena that might try to take what is ours.

God speaks a command that is biologically counter-intuitive and seemingly reckless. He commands us to go on offense. He commands us to take the resources we have painstakingly hunted and gathered, our money, our time, our emotional energy, and give them away to people who did not earn them.

This is the third pillar of our prescription. Giving is not merely a nice thing to do, it is a declaration of war against our own survival instincts. When we give, we are telling our nervous systems that the rules of the jungle no longer apply to us. We are declaring that we do not live by the scarcity of the wild, but by the abundance of the Kingdom.

PART II: THE SICKNESS OF SODOM (THE CALLOUS HEART)

To understand why this offense is necessary for our spiritual health, we must return to the diagnosis of Sodom we began in the previous chapter. In Chapter 6, we looked at the first two charges in **Ezekiel 16:49**: "Arrogant" and "Overfed." We saw how the fullness of the stomach lulled the soul to sleep, necessitating the discipline of fasting.

The verse does not end there. The diagnosis continues, drawing a straight line from their physical consumption to their social callousness. The text concludes:

> *...they were arrogant, overfed and unconcerned;*
>
> ***they did not help the poor and needy.***"
>
> ***-Ezekiel 16:49***

The Hebrew phrasing here is devastatingly specific. It literally means they did not "strengthen the hand" of the poor because their own hands were full of food and pleasure. They had no capacity to take the hand of the broken.

This reveals a troubling spiritual progression. First comes the gluttony (*Overfed*), which leads to the numbness (*Unconcerned*), which inevitably results in the hoarding (*Did not help*). When we are stuffed with our own comfort, we lose the capacity for empathy. The nervous system becomes so saturated with its own dopamine that it cannot register the pain of the neighbor.

Sodom was not destroyed because of what they did in their bedrooms. They were destroyed because they became a biological dead end. Like the Dead Sea that borders their ancient location, they took water in but let nothing flow out.

God commands us to give not because He needs our resources, but because He knows that hoarding is a toxicity. Just as unwept tears poison the brain with manganese, and unfasted gluttony poisons the body with lethargy, unshared wealth poisons the heart with a specific type of spiritual sclerosis. A heart that only pumps blood in will explode, while a heart that only pumps blood out will die. A heart that pumps in and out is alive. Giving is the systolic beat of the soul. It keeps the circulation moving, flushing out the toxicity of selfishness and preventing us from becoming a spiritual Sodom.

PART III: THE ANXIETY OF POSSESSION (THE RICH YOUNG RULER)

We see the tragedy of this defensive living most clearly in the encounter between Jesus and the Rich Young Ruler in Matthew 19 and Mark 10. This young man is the apex predator of his society. He has hunted well. He is wealthy, moral, and successful. He has played by the rules of the world and won. He comes to Jesus because he senses a deficit. Despite his hoard, he lacks the Presence. He lacks the assurance of eternal life.

> *Jesus looked at him and loved him. "One thing you lack," he said. "Go, sell everything you have and give to the poor, and you will have treasure in heaven. Then come, follow me."*
>
> ***-Mark 10:21***

Jesus, looking at him with profound love, diagnoses the blockage immediately. He sees that the young man is suffering from the anxiety of possession. The man thinks he owns his wealth, but in reality, his wealth owns him. His hands are so full of his own achievements that he has no fingers free to grasp the Kingdom.

Jesus prescribes the ultimate offense. He tells him to sell his possessions and give to the poor. This was not a financial strategy. It was a somatic intervention. Jesus was trying to break the grip. He was trying to force the young man's nervous system to let go of its security blanket so that it could finally attach to the Father.

> *At this the man's face fell. He went away sad, because he had great wealth.*
>
> ***-Mark 10:22***

The young man's reaction is heartbreaking. The text says he went away "sorrowful." The Greek implies a deep, heavy grieving. He chose the anxiety of control over the peace of surrender, and he walked away with his pockets full and his soul empty.

This is the trap of the defensive life. The more we accumulate to protect ourselves, the more we have to lose, and the more fearful we become. The fortress we build to keep the world out eventually becomes the prison that keeps us in. Giving is the only key that unlocks the door from the inside.

PART IV: THE ELDER BROTHER'S LEDGER (LUKE 15)

The struggle to give is not just about money. It is about the currency of grace. We see this vividly in the parable of the Prodigal Son in **Luke 15**. We often focus on the younger son, the wild spender who wasted his inheritance, but the story contains a darker warning in the figure of the older brother.

The older brother was obedient, but kept a ledger. He stayed home. He worked the fields. He earned his keep. He operated strictly by the law and felt justified. He is the embodiment of self-righteousness. He looks at his own sweat and concludes that he is worthy, and he looks at his brother's waste and concludes he is worthless.

When the younger brother returns, he confesses:

> *'Father, I have sinned against heaven and against you. I am no longer worthy to be called your son.'*

-Luke 15:21

The Father gives the best robe (covering the shame). He gives the ring (restoring authority). He kills the fatted calf (sacrificial celebration).

The Older Brother cannot handle this. He stands outside the feast, angry and refusing to go in. Listen to his complaint:

> *Look! All these years I've been slaving for you and never disobeyed your orders. Yet you never gave me even a young goat so I could celebrate with my friends.*

-Luke 15:28

The Older Brother has a calculator in his heart. He is counting the cost. He believes that grace must be purchased with good behavior. He looks at his brother, hungry, unclothed, and broken, and he does not see a tragedy. He believes his brother brought this on himself. He knows his brother's story, and is going to treat him accordingly. "You reap what you sow."

True giving smashes this ledger mentality. When we give to the undeserving. This is to the poor who might squander it, to the neighbor who is messy, to the sinner who has not repented, then we are stepping out of the older brother's resentment and into the Father's joy. We are acknowledging that we did not create our own blessings. We are admitting that we are just as naked and hungry in our souls as the prodigal son is in his body, and that if God gave to us while we were yet sinners, we have no right to close our hand in self-righteousness to anyone else.

PART V: THE BIOLOGY OF ABUNDANCE

When we cling to our resources in a defensive posture, our bodies release cortisol. We are in a state of low-level threat, constantly calculating survival. This creates a feedback loop of fear. We hoard because we are afraid, and we are afraid because we are alone in our hoarding.

However, when we engage in the act of giving, the brain shifts. Neuroimaging studies show that generosity lights up the mesolimbic reward pathway, releasing a cocktail of oxytocin and dopamine. This is often called the "Helper's High."

Oxytocin is the molecule of connection. It is the chemical opposite of cortisol. When oxytocin floods the system, blood pressure drops, the heart rate slows, and the fight or flight mechanism disengages. The body receives a powerful signal of safety and connection.

By giving, we are hacking our own biology. We are forcing the brain to shift from a scarcity mindset to an abundance mindset . You cannot give sacrificially and remain in a state of panic. The two states are biologically incompatible. To open the hand is to tell the amygdala that the emergency is over. It is to walk in the *"cool of the day"* confidence that there is more where that came from because Our Provider is with us.

PART VI: THE SOMATIC THEOLOGY OF THE NEIGHBOR

This biological shift paves the way for the ultimate spiritual reality. Love. The Bible never speaks of love as a mere sentiment, it speaks of love as an action, specifically the action of giving.

In Ephesians 5, Paul commands us to *"walk in the way of love, just as Christ loved us and gave himself up for us."* The model is Christ and the Church. Christ did not love the Church by hoarding His divinity. He loved her by spending it. He gave His body, His blood, and His glory. He paid the ultimate sacrifice to give life to the dead.

When we give to our neighbor, we are enacting this somatic theology. We are using our physical resources to bless another physical body. This is why Jesus connects the "*Second Great Commandment*" in ***Matthew 22***

> *And the second is like it: 'Love your neighbor as yourself.'*
>
> ***-Matthew 22:39***

with the somatic act of caring for the "*Least of These*" in **Matthew 25.**

> *'Truly I tell you, whatever you did not do for one of the least of these, you did not do for me.'*
>
> ***-Matthew 25:45***

When we feed the hungry, we are not just solving a caloric deficit, we are affirming their dignity. When we clothe the naked, we are covering their shame, as God did in the Garden of Eden. When we give to the poor, we are loving our neighbor not with abstract thoughts, but with concrete sacrifice.

This connects directly to the peace we seek. You can not be at peace with your neighbor if you are watching him suffer.

By giving, we dismantle the walls of suspicion and competition. We stop seeing the neighbor as a "hyena" trying to steal our kill, and start seeing them as a brother trying to find his way home.

PART VII: THE FLOW OF THE RIVER

We must be careful to distinguish this type of giving from the transactional heresy that permeates so much of modern religion. We are not talking about investing in God to get a return. That is just capitalism in a cassock. That is still the defensive instinct, trying to manipulate God to secure more resources for the hoard.

True giving, the giving of the sackcloth prescription, is about release. It is about flow. It is the recognition that we are not the source of the water. We are merely the pipes. If a pipe tries to hold onto the water, it bursts. If it lets the water flow, it stays fresh.

God commands us to give because He wants to save us from the stagnation of Sodom and the sorrow of the Rich Young Ruler. He wants to save us from the exhausting, lonely work of defending our little kingdom. He invites us to join the economy of Heaven, where the more you give, the more you have, and where the open hand is the only hand that can hold the hand of the Father.

So we give. We give until it scares us. We give until the "Mine!" reflex dies. In that death, we find abundant life. We find that we are no longer scavengers fighting for scraps, but sons and daughters seated at a table that is never empty.

Now that the hand is open, the stomach is empty, and the tears have cleared the eyes, the vessel is finally ready. We have silenced the noise of the body and the noise of the world. We are ready to enter the final chamber. We are ready to shut the door and speak to the Father in the Secret Place.

Chapter 8:

The Secret Place (Prayer)

PART I: THE REWARD OF THE ROOM

We have arrived at the fourth and final pillar of the prescription.We have explored the House of Mourning (Lament). We have entered the discipline of the Empty Stomach (Fasting). We have practiced the rebellion of the Open Hand (Giving). Now, we enter the **Secret Place**.

In **Matthew 6**, Jesus follows a specific rhythm. He addresses Giving, then Prayer, then Fasting. In each section, He contrasts two types of people: the Performer and the Child.

> *And when you pray, do not be like the hypocrites, for they love to pray standing in the synagogues and on the street corners to be seen by others. Truly I tell you, they have received their reward in full.*
>
> ***-Matthew 6:5***

The Performer prays for notoriety. Their goal is social capital. They want to be known as "spiritual." They use eloquent words, perfect theology, and public displays to curate an image. And Jesus say:

"They got what they wanted. They got the likes. They got the applause. That is the only reward they will ever see."

Then He pivots to the prescription for Presence:

> *But when you pray, go into your room, close the door and pray to your Father, who is unseen. Then your Father, who sees what is done in secret, will reward you.*
>
> ***-Matthew 6:6***

The Greek word for "room" here is *tameion*. It refers to an inner chamber, a storage closet, or a secret storehouse. It is the most private place in the home. It is a place where there is no audience.

Jesus insists on the closet because you cannot impress people and connect with God at the same time. As long as the door is open, you are performing. You are editing your words. You are conscious of your posture. You are thinking about how you sound, but when the door clicks shut, the performance dies. In the secret place, there is no one to clap. There is no one to judge. It is just you and the Father.

This is where the liquid language is spoken most fluently. This is where the mask comes off. This is where we stop reciting prayers and start becoming prayer.

PART II: THE BODY LEADS THE MIND (EMBODIED COGNITION)

For centuries, we have treated prayer as a mental exercise. We sit in comfortable chairs, close our eyes, and try to think holy thoughts, but this ignores the fundamental design of the human vessel. We are not brains in jars. We are embodied souls.

Modern neuroscience has discovered a principle called **Embodied Cognition**. The brain is not the only thing that thinks. The way you arrange your physical limbs, the rhythm of your breath, and the position of your spine send powerful signals back to your brain, instructing it on how to feel and what to believe.

The Body leads. The Mind follows.

If you are slouching, crossing your arms, and frowning, your body is sending a signal to your brain that says, "We are closed off." "We are defensive." It is neurologically difficult to pray a prayer of surrender while your body is in a posture of defense. This is why the Bible speaks on posture. In biblical times they did not just "think" their prayers. They enacted them. They knelt. They lifted hands. They fell on their faces. They stood with heads bowed.

PART III: THE GEOMETRY OF SURRENDER

Let's look at the science behind three specific biblical postures of prayer. These are not arbitrary rituals. They are biological switches.

1. Kneeling (The Signal of Safety)

Kneeling is a signal of immobilization. When we are in the sympathetic fight or flight mode, our legs are primed with blood flow. We are ready to run. We are mobile. We are autonomous. When you kneel, you mechanically disadvantage your own escape system. You fold your legs under you. You lower your center of gravity. You ground yourself. To the primitive brain (the amygdala), this is out of order. You have made yourself defenseless, but because you are doing it voluntarily, the signal changes. By overriding the instinct to run, you are sending a massive signal to your nervous system that you are safe and have no need to flee.

Kneeling down regulates the stress response. It tells the anxiety to stand down. Your testosterone level drops and aggression fades. Your heart rate slows and the fight for survival silents. Your focus narrows, reducing distraction. You kneel not because you are already humble. You kneel to become humble. The posture leads the heart.

2. Raising Hands (The Signal of Vulnerability)

This is often the most difficult posture for people, especially men. It feels awkward. It feels vulnerable. That is exactly the point.

Anatomically, when you lift your arms above your head, you expose your **kill zone**. You lift your arms away from your rib cage, exposing the heart, the lungs, and the soft tissue of the throat and underarms. In a physical fight, this is suicide. Our instinct when threatened is the fetal position by curling inward to protect the vitals. To raise your hands is to override the deepest survival instinct of the mammal. In battle you are saying: "I am unarmed. I surrender."

This physical vulnerability often triggers the emotional release we discussed in Chapter 1. This is why people often start crying the moment they lift their hands. They have physically unlocked the cage where they were hiding their heart. They are telling the Lord: "I trust you." "I surrender."

3. Prostration (The Signal of Ego Death)

There is one final posture, rarely practiced in today's church, but ubiquitous in the Bible. Falling face down. This is **prostration**. In Hebrew, the word often translated as "worship" is *shachah*. It literally means "to depress," "to bow down," or "to fall flat."

Biologically, prostration is a form of self-induced sensory

deprivation. Your vision is cut off. You only see the ground. Your sound is muffled. Your ears are turned toward the earth. Your movement stops. You are anchored. Psychologically, this is the posture of **ego death**. The world has narrowed down to the rhythm of your own breath and the dust against your forehead.

It is the physical enactment of "hitting rock bottom," and for the nervous system, hitting bottom is sometimes the only way to stop the spinning. When the brain is overwhelmed with the "Toxic Load" of Chapter 2, prostration acts as a grounding wire. It maximizes the contact surface between the body and the earth. It is full surrender.

PART IV: THE SILENCE OF THE SECRET PLACE

So, we enter the room. We close the door. We kneel or fall on our faces. What do we say?

Sometimes, nothing.

In **Romans 8:26**, Paul gives us a lifeline for the moments when the trauma is too heavy for words:

> *In the same way, the Spirit helps us in our weakness. We do not know what we ought to pray*

for, but the Spirit himself intercedes for us through ***wordless groans.***

-Romans 8:26

This connects back to the Shutdown of Broca's Area (Chapter 1). When we are in deep pain, or deep awe, our speech center goes offline. We literally cannot find the words.

In the street corner prayer in *Matthew 6:5*, the goal is eloquence. The Pharisee wants to have the best words.

"And when you pray, do not be like the hypocrites, for they love to pray standing in the synagogues and on the street corners to be seen by others. Truly I tell you, they have received their reward in full."

In the secret place prayer in *Matthew 6:6*, the goal is honesty. If you can not speak, you groan. If you can not groan, you weep. If you can not weep, you breathe. He takes the raw data of your "weakness", of your confusion, of your exhaustion, of your tears, and translates them into words. This is the freedom of the Secret Place. You don't have to be a poet. You just have to be present.

PART V: THE SYNTHESIS (THE WHOLE VESSEL)

We can now see how the four pillars work together as a single, integrated system for restoring His Presence. When we **Lament** we clear the emotional debris, releasing the toxic load of grief and sorrow. When we **Fast** we clear the biological noise, removing the dopamine buffer of food, resulting in a sharper mind. When we **Give** we clear the anxiety of control, releasing the grip of greed and fear, which results in surrendering our will. So, when we **Pray** in the secret place we have a point of connection, with the posture of surrender and honest communication, resulting in the **Presence of the Lord.**

When these four are operating, the vessel is clean. The static is gone. The interference is removed. We are no longer the "Overfed and Unconcerned" people of Sodom. We are no longer the "Tearless Men" like Cain. We are no longer the "Rich Young Rulers" holding onto our control. We are empty. We are open. We are grounded. When the human soul is emptied of self, God rushes in to fill the space.

PART VI: THE REWARD IS THE PERSON

The "Reward" Jesus promised in Matthew 6 is not a thing. It is not a check in the mail. It is not a platform. The Reward is **Him**. The Reward is the restoration of the walk in the Garden. It is the peace of knowing you are fully known and fully loved. It is the quieting of the internal war. It is peace.

When we practice these disciplines, we are not paying the price for a miracle. We are simply following the Manufacturer's Instructions for the human machine. When we lament, we are changing the oil. When we fast, we are cleaning the filter. When we give, we are opening the valve. When we pray, we are connecting the power source. We do it because we want the engine to run. We do it because we want to live life more abundantly.

There is one final piece of the puzzle. We have talked about clearing the vessel, but what happens to the tears we shed? Do they just evaporate into the carpet of the secret place, or are they going somewhere?

In the next part of this book, we are going to look at the **restoration**. We are going to find out that God is not just a passive observer of our discipline. He is an active collector of our pain. He keeps a bottle, and He is writing a book.

Chapter 9: The God Who Collects

PART I: THE BREAKING POINT

There is a breaking point in human suffering where language fails. We have all been there. You are kneeling by a bedside in a hospital room, the hum of the machines filling the silence. You are sitting in your car in a parking lot, gripping the steering wheel until your knuckles turn white. You are lying on the floor of your bedroom in the middle of the night, staring at the ceiling fan.

You want to pray. You know you should pray. You have practiced the Secret Place (Chapter 8). You have entered the room and closed the door, but now that you are there, the words will not come.

Your mind is a whirlwind of grief, panic, and confusion. The thoughts are desperate, but the mechanism that turns those thoughts into sentences has jammed. You try to say, "God, please..." or "Why..." but the sentence fractures before it finishes. You are left in a heavy, suffocating silence, perhaps able only to heave a sigh or let out a guttural groan.

In many religious traditions, and certainly in the modern culture of "articulate faith," this moment is viewed as a spiritual failure. We judge ourselves harshly for it. We assume that if we can not present a coherent case to the Judge, the Judge can not hear us. We believe that God speaks in languages we understand, and if we are not broadcasting on that frequency, we are talking to the void.

The intersection of neurobiology and theology tells a very different story. The science of trauma reveals that the absence of words is not a lack of faith. It is a neurological necessity. It is what happens to a human brain when it is operating at the limit of its capacity, and the Bible tells us that God is not only aware of this limitation. He designed a workaround for it.

He designed the **Liquid Language**.

In this chapter, we are going to explore the Theology of the Bottle. We are going to look at the God who does not require words, the Spirit who translates groans, and the divine act of collecting the prayers that fall from our eyes.

PART II: THE NEUROSCIENCE OF THE SHUTDOWN

To understand why we lose our words when we hurt, we have to look at the geography of the brain. Specifically, we must look at the fragile relationship between the Amygdala and Broca's Area.

The human brain is an energy-efficient machine. It directs blood flow and oxygen to the areas that are working the hardest. The **Broca's Area** is located in the left frontal lobe, this is the speech center of the brain. It is responsible for translating your abstract thoughts and feelings into spoken language. When you are writing an email, ordering coffee, or chatting with a friend, Broca's Area is lit up with activity. It is the sophisticated editor of your mind.

The **Amygdala** is located deep in the temporal lobe, this is the brain's smoke detector. It scans for threat, fear, and danger. In a normal, low-stress environment, these two areas communicate well. You can feel a mild emotion (Amygdala) and describe it with words (Broca's Area). When significant trauma or overwhelming emotion hits like a sudden death, a betrayal, a diagnosis, a moment of terror, the brain undergoes a radical shift in resource allocation.

Because survival is the priority, the brain shunts blood flow and oxygen away from the higher-order thinking centers (the frontal lobes) and floods the primal survival centers. The Amygdala hijacks the system. One of the first casualties of this hijack is Broca's Area.

Dr. Bessel van der Kolk, one of the world's leading trauma researchers, has shown through neuroimaging that when people are recalling a traumatic event, Broca's Area effectively goes offline. It shuts down. The lights go out. This condition is called **Speechless Terror**.

It explains why, immediately after a car accident, victims often stand around in stunned silence, unable to answer simple questions from police officers. It explains why a grieving widow might sit at a funeral reception for hours, staring into space, unable to form a sentence.

The bridge between feeling and speaking has been washed out by the flood of stress hormones. The data is stuck in the emotional center. It can not cross the river to the speech center.

In prayer, if God demanded articulate sentences as the price of admission to His Presence, then the most hurting people on earth would be the most cut off from Him. The very moment you need God the most during trauma is the moment you are biologically least capable of talking to Him. This would be a cruel design, but God is not cruel. He knows our frame. He remembers that we are dust (**Psalm 103:14**). Because He knows our biology, He has provided a spiritual fail-safe.

> *for he knows how we are formed, he remembers that we are dust.*
>
> ***-Psalm 103:14***

PART III: THE FUGITIVE'S PRAYER

To understand this fail-safe in action, we must return to the life of David. David is our guide through this book because he embodies the full spectrum of the human experience. He is the warrior and the weeper. He is the king and the fugitive.

There is a moment in David's life that is arguably his lowest point. It is recorded in **1 Samuel 21**, and the corresponding song is **Psalm 56**.

David is on the run from King Saul, who wants to kill him. In a moment of desperation, he flees into enemy territory, Gath, the hometown of Goliath. It is a terrible miscalculation. The servants of the King of Gath recognize him immediately. They say, *"Isn't this David? The one they sing about? The one who killed our champion?"* David realizes he is trapped. He is surrounded by enemies who have every reason to torture and execute him. He is terrified. The Bible says he was so afraid that he changed his behavior before them and feigned madness. He scratched at the doors of the gate and let saliva run down his beard.

Imagine the anointed King of Israel, the sweet psalmist, is now scratching at wood like an animal, drooling, eyes wide with panic. He has lost his dignity. He has lost his composure. He has lost his words. Broca's Area has shut down. He is in survival mode.

Later, when he processes this event in the Secret Place,

he writes **Psalm 56**. In verse 8, he reveals what was happening in the spiritual realm while he was drooling in the physical realm.

> *You keep track of all my sorrows. You have collected all my tears in your bottle. Are they not in your record?*
>
> ***-Psalm 56:8***

Let's unpack the three distinct images David uses here. They reveal the theology of the God who collects.

1. The Wanderings (*Nod*) The first phrase, *"You keep track of all my sorrows,"* can also be translated as *"You number my wanderings"* or *"You count my tossings."* The Hebrew word is *Nod*. It refers to the restless movement of a fugitive. It is the pacing back and forth in a cell. It is the tossing and turning in bed at 3:00 AM when anxiety will not let you sleep.

David is saying: *God, you have a pedometer on my anxiety. You know every step I have taken in fear. You know every hour of sleep I have lost.* God is paying attention to the physical agitation of his body.

2. The Bottle (*No'd*) Then comes the central image: *"Put* *my tears in your bottle."*

The Hebrew word here is *No'd* (a play on words with *Nod*). To understand this, we have to look at the archaeology of the Ancient Near East. If you were to excavate an ancient tomb in Israel, Rome, or Persia, you might find small vessels made of glass or ceramic. They have long, thin necks and bulbous bottoms. These are known as *Lachrymatories*, or "Tear Bottles." The tradition was poignant. When a loved one died, the mourners would not just weep into the dust. They would press these small bottles against their cheeks to catch the tears as they fell.

Why? In an arid landscape, water is precious, but water shed for love is the most precious substance of all. To collect a tear was to say: "This grief is valuable. This loss matters. I am not ashamed of how much I loved this person."

Often, these bottles would be corked and buried with the deceased. In some traditions, they were kept by the family as a memorial. By using this imagery, David is asking God to treat his tears as a survival ration, but more than that, he is making a statement about **intimacy**.

Think about the physics of catching a tear in a bottle. You

can not do it from a distance. You cannot do it from across the room. To catch a tear, you have to be right next to the person's face. You have to be close enough to feel their breath. You have to be close enough to touch their skin. David is dismantling the idea of a distant God. He is describing a God who is hovering within millimeters of his cheek, catching the runoff of his pain.

3. The Book (*Sepher*) Finally, David asks: *"Are they not in your record?"* The word is *Sepher*. It means a scroll, a book, or a ledger. David shifts the metaphor from a Bottle of preservation to a Book of accounting. He views God as a **Biographer**. This implies that God is keeping a ledger of human suffering. Every moment of grief that the world ignores, God records. Every silent weep in the shower that no spouse or friend witnesses, God writes down.

God keeps these records because God is a God of Justice. In biblical times, kings kept records of debts and favors. If someone was harmed, it was written in the book so that restitution could be made. By asking "Are they not in your book?" David is saying: "God, I know you are keeping score. I know that this pain is not meaningless. I know that one day, you will open the book, and you will right these wrongs."

PART IV: THE TRANSLATOR SPIRIT

What happens to the tears once they are collected?

They are translated. This is where the liquid language becomes literal. As we discussed in Chapter 1, tears contain biological data (ACTH, manganese, leucine enkephalin). They carry the chemical signature of our stress, but in the spiritual realm, they carry the signature of our heart. When Broca's Area is shut down, the Holy Spirit steps in as the Divine Translator.

Paul describes this mechanism in **Romans 8:26-27**:

> *In the same way, the Spirit helps us in our weakness. We do not know what we ought to pray for, but the Spirit himself intercedes for us through* ***wordless groans****. And he who searches our hearts knows the mind of the Spirit, because the Spirit intercedes for God's people in accordance with the will of God.*
>
> ***-Romans 8:26-27***

Notice the phrase **"wordless groans."** This is the sound

of the Glottis opening inChapter 3. It is the sound of the deep, guttural wail. It is the sound of the liquid language flowing. The text says that the Spirit *intercedes* through these groans. This means that your breakdown is actually a breakthrough. When you are lying on the floor, weeping and unable to speak, you are not failing to pray. You are providing the raw data.

You are providing the tears, the cortisol, the heartbreak, and the confusion. The Holy Spirit takes that raw data and encodes it into a perfect prayer that aligns with the will of God, and God receives it.

PART V: THE EMPATHY OF THE WITNESS (THE GOD WHO FEELS)

This theology of the "Bottle and the Book" validates the helpless ache we often feel when watching others suffer. We have all been in situations where we were powerless to fix a tragedy. You can not cure the cancer eating away at a friend. You can not bring back the spouse your sister lost. You cannot erase the trauma of someone's past. You stand on the sidelines, helpless to change their reality. In those moments, when your hands are empty of solutions, your eyes often fill with tears. All you can do is cry.

You weep because you are feeling their weight. You are simulating their grief in your own body. You are collecting their pain in your own heart. That empathy, that shared ache, is the closest we ever come to the image of God.

God is the ultimate Empath. He does not just know about our suffering in an intellectual sense of His omniscience. He feels our suffering in a relational sense through His compassion. When we are heartbroken, He is not analyzing the data. He is carrying the load.

When we cry, we are tapping into this divine nature. We are vibrating at His frequency. This is why the **Secret Place** in Chapter 8 is so vital. When you go into the room and close the door, you are not just escaping the world, you are entering the collection center. You are entering the place where the bottle is kept.

If you skip the Secret Place by staying busy, staying strong, or staying distracted, you are denying God the opportunity to collect your tears. You are letting them evaporate in the wind of busyness. You are wasting your pain. Do not waste your pain. Every drop of it is precious to Him. Every drop of it is a sentence in the book that He is writing about your life.

PART VI: THE VALIDATION OF THE INVISIBLE WAR

This chapter is particularly important for those whose suffering is invisible.

There is a type of grief that gets a lot of public support like the death of a spouse, a cancer diagnosis, or a house fire. People bring casseroles. They send cards. The suffering is public and validated.

The miscarriage that no one knew about. The slow, grinding pain of a loveless marriage. The exhaustion of caring for a special needs child or an aging parent. The loneliness of leadership. The battle with chronic mental illness. The "John Henry" weight of carrying a community that expects you to be strong. This grief happens in the dark. There are no funerals for it. There are no casseroles. You cry alone in the car, and then you fix your makeup and go into the meeting. You feel invisible. You feel like your pain does not count because no one sees it.

Psalm 56 is the anthem for the invisible sufferer. The audience of the Lord is enough. Even if no human being ever sees your sacrifice, even if no one ever validates your pain, God has the bottle. He has the book. He has not missed a single frame of the movie.

This validation allows us to keep going. We do not need the applause of the crowd or the pity of the tribe if we know that the King has the record.

PART VII: THE PRESENCE RESTORED

When we pour out the liquid language, and God collects it, the space inside us is cleared. The manganese is gone. The cortisol is flushed, and in that clean, empty space, the presence of the Lord settles. This is the peace that surpasses understanding. It is not the peace of "everything is fixed." It is the peace of "I am known."

It is the realization that you are not crying into the void. You are crying into a bottle held by the Creator of the Universe. We have seen the God who collects the tears, but does He ever shed them? Does the God of the Universe speak the liquid language Himself?

In the next chapter, we will walk into Bethany. We will see the Creator in the flesh, and we will see that when He encountered the grief of His friends, He did not just offer a theology.

He offered a tear.

Chapter 10:

The Incarnation of Empathy

PART I: THE SHORTEST VERSE, THE DEEPEST TRUTH

It is the shortest verse in the English Bible. It consists of only two words, nine letters.

John 11:35: "Jesus wept."

Because of its brevity, it is often treated as a footnote. It is the verse children memorize in Sunday School to get an easy prize.. It is the verse we gloss over to get to the part where the dead man walks out of the tomb. If we place these two words under the microscope of both theology and neurobiology we discover that they contain the entire justification for human emotion. They are the fulcrum upon which the Christian understanding of pain rests.

If you remove this verse from the Bible, you change the nature of God. You are left with a God who solves problems but does not feel them. You are left with a Greek Stoic deity who pulls strings from the heavens but remains untouched by the agony of the earth. John 11:35 gives us a God with a face, a God with a nervous system, and a God with a lacrimal gland.

In this chapter, we will walk into Bethany, and look at the biological reality of the Incarnation. We will ask the difficult question: *Why did the Man who knew the solution still feel the need to cry?*

PART II: THE CONTEXT OF THE CATASTROPHE

To understand the weight of Jesus' tears, we must first understand the thickness of the despair He walked into. Lazarus is dead. He is not just freshly dead, he has been in the tomb for four days.

This four day detail is not accidental. In the ancient Jewish tradition, there was a belief that the soul of the deceased hovered over the body for three days, attempting to re-enter. There was a superstitious hope that perhaps the person was not really dead, and that they might wake up from a coma or a swoon.

By the fourth day, hope was extinguished. By the fourth day, the face began to change, decomposition set in and the body began to bloat. The smell of death became undeniable. This is why Martha, ever the pragmatist, warns Jesus in verse 39: *"Lord, by this time there is a bad odor, for he has been there four days."* The situation is not critical, it is irreversible. It is biologically final.

When Jesus arrives in Bethany, the village is in chaos. Mary and Martha, the sisters of Lazarus, are wrecking balls of sorrow. They have not slept. They have not eaten. They are operating on pure cortisol and adrenaline, and they are angry. Both sisters greet Jesus with the exact same accusation: *"Lord, if you had been here, my brother would not have died."* It is a theological indictment. This is the atmosphere Jesus walks into. It is a wall of sound, a wall of smell, and a wall of accusation. It is the rawest, ugliest version of human suffering.

PART III: THE OMNISCIENCE PARADOX

Here is where the theological tension snaps tight because Jesus knows the end of the story. Before He even left for Bethany, He told His disciples explicitly: *"Lazarus is dead, and for your sake I am glad I was not there, so that you may believe."* He knows He is going to wake him up.

He knows that in roughly ten minutes, He is going to walk over to the limestone cave, shout "*Come out!*", and Lazarus is going to shuffle out, alive and well. He has the ultimate solution in His back pocket.

If a parent sees a child crying over a broken toy, and the parent knows they have a brand new, identical toy hidden behind their back, the parent usually smiles. They might feel a tender sympathy, but they do not fall to the floor and sob. They present the new toy and instantly tears turn to smiles.

We expect Jesus to be the smiling Savior. We expect Him to walk into Bethany, hold up his hand to silence the wailing, and say, *"Come out!"* and everyone would rejoice. That would be efficient. That would be powerful. It would prove His divinity.

Instead, the text says that when He saw Mary weeping, and the Jews who had come along with her also weeping, He was *"deeply moved in spirit and troubled."* And then, He wept. What we would call a waste of time, He knew was essential. He delayed the miracle to fully embrace the grief. Jesus had 100% hope. He had 100% certainty of victory, and yet, He still had 100% sorrow. This teaches us a fundamental lesson about the nature of tears. That the solution does not cancel the sorrow.

Just because things will be okay in the end during the resurrection does not mean they are okay right now during times of death. The hope of the future does not erase the pain of the present. Jesus refused to use His theology to bypass His humanity.

PART IV: THE MIRROR NEURONS OF GOD

Why did He do it? If He knew Lazarus was coming back, what triggered the tears?

The text gives us the specific trigger in verse 33: *"When Jesus* ***saw her weeping****, and the Jews who had come along with her also weeping, he was deeply moved..."* He didn't cry because

Lazarus was dead. He cried because Mary was crying. This is the ultimate validation of the **Mirror Neuron** system.

Neuroscience tells us that the human brain contains a specialized set of neurons that fire both when we perform an action and when we observe someone else performing that same action. If I smile, my motor neurons fire. If I see you smile, those same neurons in my brain fire, as if I were smiling myself. This is the biological hardware of empathy. It is the system that allows us to feel what another person is feeling.

Jesus possessed a fully human brain. He had a prefrontal cortex, an amygdala, and a mirror neuron system. When He looked into the face of Mary and saw the contortion of her grief, His biology responded exactly the way a healthy human biology is designed to respond with resonance.

He simulated her pain in His own mind. He allowed her agony to become His agony. This is a stunning theological reversal. Religion usually teaches *Imitatio Christi* or that humans should imitate Christ. The Incarnation shows us God imitating man.

By weeping when Mary wept, Jesus was *"weeping with those who weep"* **Romans 12:15**. He was allowing the external signal of her distress to penetrate His internal fortress. This proves that empathy is more important to God than efficiency.

If Jesus cared only about efficiency, He would have raised Lazarus immediately. That would have stopped the crying instantly. It would have been the quickest way to fix the problem, but Jesus prioritized connection over solution. He knew that if He fixed the problem without validating the pain, He would not have been a Savior. A Savior enters reality to be with you.

By stopping to weep, Jesus was saying to Mary: *"I am going to fix this, but before I fix it, I need you to know that I feel it. I am not skipping over your pain. I am sitting in it with you."* This was no passive, polite display of sorrow. The Greek word used to describe His emotional state is *embrimaomai*, a shuddering, visceral groan often translated as the snorting of a warhorse. It is a physical, violent indignation against death itself. In that moment, the mirror neurons of God fully engaged with human trauma, proving that the body's physical release of grief is a necessity. He did not bypass the pain. He anchored His divine power to raise the dead in His profound willingness to first weep for the dead.

PART V: THE GOD OF THE FUNERAL

This scene dismantles the heresy of Docetism or Gnosticism, which plagued the early church and still infects us today. These ancient heresies argued that Jesus only appeared to be human, or that His physical body was an illusion, a costume He wore while His real divine spirit remained aloof. If Jesus were merely a divine spirit, He would not have cried. Spirits do not have hormones. Spirits don't have lacrimal glands. Spirits do not get headaches from sobbing. John 11:35 is the proof of the flesh. It proves that God has a nervous system.

It means God knows the sensation of the lump in the throat. He knows the stinging pressure behind the eyes. He knows the exhaustion that follows a sob. He knows the salt on the lips.

This changes how we pray. When we are suffering, we are not praying to a distant cosmic force who has read a textbook about pain. We are praying to a God who has the scars of trauma in His memory. When we tell Him, "Lord, it hurts," He does not say, "I can imagine." He says, "I remember."

PART VI: THE TEARLESS HERESY

This brings us to a confrontation with modern Christian culture. If Christ being the Perfect Man and the only human being who ever lived without sin, wept openly and violently in public, then why do we consider composure to be a sign of holiness?

We have internalized a stoic version of Christianity. We believe that faith means being unflappable. We think that if we trust God, we will not cry at the funeral. We think that if we are "full of the Spirit," we will always be smiling.

If Jesus wept, then a tearless Christianity is a Christ-less Christianity. If we refuse to weep, we are claiming to be stronger than Jesus. We are claiming a level of emotional control that God Himself did not practice. In fact, the Gospels suggest that the inability to respond emotionally is a sign of hardness, not holiness. Jesus frequently got angry at the Pharisees for their *"hardness of heart."* They were the ones who kept their composure. They were the ones who cared more about the rules and the optics than the human suffering in front of them.

Jesus was the messiest person in the room at Bethany. He was the one shaking. He was the one snorting with rage. He was the one leaking fluid, and in that mess, He was revealing the glory of God.

This gives us permission to be human. It validates our grief. It tells us that our tears are not a failure of faith, they are an act of *Imitatio Christi*. When we weep over the brokenness of the world, we are standing exactly where Jesus stood.

PART VII: THE ULTIMATE SOMATIC EVENT (GETHSEMANE)

Bethany was not the peak of Jesus' somatic suffering. It was only the prelude. To fully understand the Incarnation of Tears, we must fast-forward a few days to a garden at the foot of the Mount of Olives in Gethsemane.

Here, the stress load on the human body of Jesus moves critical. He is facing the Cross, but more than the physical torture, He is facing the cup of God's wrath. The spiritual separation from the Father that sin demands.

The emotional weight of this is so heavy that the Gospel writers struggle to describe it. Matthew says He began to be *"sorrowful and troubled"* (26:37). Mark says He was *"deeply distressed and horrified"* (14:33). Jesus Himself says, *"My soul is overwhelmed with sorrow to the point of death"* (Matthew

26:38).

This is a biological statement. He is saying, *The stress is so high that it is about to kill me, even before I get to the cross,* and then, Luke, the physician, records the physiological result of this pressure:

> *And being in anguish, he prayed more earnestly, and his sweat was like drops of blood falling to the ground.*
>
> ***-Luke 22:44***

For centuries, skeptics dismissed this as a metaphor, but modern medicine recognizes this as a rare but documented condition called **Hematohidrosis**. Hematohidrosis occurs only under conditions of extreme, life-threatening stress. When the fight or flight system is pushed beyond its maximum limit, the capillaries that feed the sweat glands rupture. The blood mixes with the sweat and is pushed out through the pores. This is the ultimate somatic response. The body is under so much pressure that it begins to weep blood.

This proves, once and for all, that Jesus held nothing back. He did not use His divinity to shield His biology. He did not turn on a "God Mode" cheat code to numb the pain. He let the full weight of the trauma crush His human nervous system until the blood vessels burst. He took the raw material of all our grief, all our shame, all our trauma, and He processed it through the machinery of His own body.

He became the Refinery. In the Garden of Eden, the first Adam sinned in a garden and brought sweat to the brow of mankind: *"By the sweat of your brow you shall eat food."* In the Garden of Gethsemane, the Second Adam obeyed in a garden and sweat blood to redeem mankind.

The tear of Bethany and the blood-sweat of Gethsemane are the same fluid. They are the evidence of a God who went to the absolute limit of physical and emotional endurance to be with us.

PART VIII: THE FELLOWSHIP OF SUFFERING

There is a profound comfort in the weeping Christ. When we are in the depths of our own disorientation, (**Psalm 13**) we often feel abandoned. We feel like God is high above, watching us struggle, but the doctrine of the Incarnation says he is with us in that moment.

He is not watching the funeral from the balcony, He is sitting in the front row, weeping. He is not analyzing our panic attack from a distance, He is kneeling in the garden, sweating blood with us.

The Apostle Paul calls this *"the fellowship of sharing in his sufferings"* **Philippians 3:10**. When we cry, we are not entering a place where God is absent. We are entering the very emotional space that Jesus occupied most deeply. We are sharing a language with Him. The liquid language. When you weep for a lost loved one, you are in fellowship with the Jesus of Bethany. When you weep over the injustice of the world, you are in fellowship with the Jesus of Jerusalem. When you weep from the sheer terrifying weight of obedience, you are in fellowship with the Jesus of Gethsemane. Your tears are a point of contact. They are the place where your humanity touches His humanity.

Conclusion: The Holy Water

In the Catholic and Orthodox traditions, there is a practice of using Holy Water to bless, to cleanse, and to sanctify. The Incarnation teaches us that the holiest water is not found in a font at the front of the church. It is found in the eyes of a suffering believer.

Jesus made tears holy by shedding them. He sanctified the act of weeping. He turned the biological reflex of the lacrimal gland into a sacrament. So, the next time you feel the tears coming, whether they are tears of grief, rage, or exhaustion, do not wipe them away in shame. Do not apologize for being emotional. You are doing exactly what your Savior did. You are letting the truth flow.

You are functioning as a human being, made in the image of a God who knows how to cry, but the story of the tear does not end with grief. The tear has one final, miraculous function. It is not just a release for the self, it is a solvent for the enemy. It is the only fluid capable of washing away the stain of betrayal.

We must now move from the Tears of Trauma to the Tears of Reconciliation. We must enter the difficult, beautiful biology of Forgiveness, and look at the biblical day when the High Priest would enter the Holy of Holies to wipe the slate clean.

Chapter 11:

The Biology of Forgiveness (Yom Kippur)

PART I: THE FINAL TOXIN

We have traversed the valley of grief through Lament, the desert of hunger through Fasting, and the vulnerability of the open hand through Giving. We have knelt in the Secret Place and learned to speak the liquid language.

The vessel is almost clean, but there is one final, stubborn stain that often refuses to lift. It is the hardest toxin to flush because, unlike grief or hunger, it often feels good to hold onto it. It feels protective. It feels like justice. It is **The Grudge**.

Forgiveness is often sold to us as a high-minded moral duty. We view it as a legal transaction where someone owes us a debt, and we sign a document canceling that debt. We think of it as an act of will. We grit our teeth, look the offender in the eye, and say, "I forgive you," while every cell in our body screams in protest, but if you have ever tried to forgive a deep betrayal like infidelity, abuse, or slander, you know that signing the document in your mind does not stop the pain in your gut. You can say the words a thousand times, but your heart still races when you see their name on your phone. You still dream about revenge. You still feel the phantom limb of the relationship that was cut off. This is because forgiveness is not just a legal decision, it is a biological event.

True reconciliation requires more than a change of mind, it requires a change of physiology. It requires the nervous system to switch from "Defense" to "Safety." It requires the blood chemistry to shift from "War" to "Peace, and almost without exception, this biological shift is marked by the shedding of tears.

In this chapter, we will explore the Anatomy of the Grudge and the ancient wisdom of Yom Kippur (The Day of Atonement). We will see how the High Priest used a goat to do what our bodies need to do with trauma, and we will look at the dramatic reunion of two brothers who washed away twenty years of hatred with a single embrace.

PART II: THE ANATOMY OF THE TORTURERS

To understand the miracle of forgiveness, we must first understand the biology of the enemy. When you are hurt by someone your brain encodes that person as a predator.

This is a survival mechanism. The Amygdala (the threat detection center) takes a snapshot of the offender. It records their face, their voice, and the context of the injury. It tags this file as danger.

From that moment on, whenever you think of that person, or see them, or hear their name, your body automatically initiates the stress response. Your cortisol spikes. Your muscles tighten preparing for a fight. Your digestion halts. Your immune system suppresses. This is the state of unforgiveness.

Biologically, a grudge is not a passive memory. It is an

active, caloric-burning state of Chronic Defensive Arousal. You are essentially freezing the moment of the injury in time. You are walking around in a permanent defensive crouch, waiting for the next blow. The problem is that the blow never comes. The event is over, but your body does mpt know that.

In **Matthew 18**, Jesus tells the Parable of the Unmerciful Servant. It is a story of a servant who is forgiven a massive debt by his master, but he refuses to forgive a small debt owed to him by a fellow servant. When the master finds out, he is furious.

> *In anger his master handed him over to the jailers to be* ***tortured****, until he should pay back all he owed.*
>
> ***-Matthew 18:34***

Theologically, this is a warning about divine judgment, but biologically, it is a description of immediate reality. When you refuse to forgive, you are not punishing the other person. You are handing yourself over to the torturers.

The torturers are your own stress hormones. The Torture of the Stomach is chronic cortisol eats away at the stomach lining, causing ulcers, acid reflux, and IBS. The Torture of the Heart is constant hypertension hardens the arteries, leading to heart disease and stroke. The Torture of the Mind is th elevated norepinephrine prevents deep sleep, leading to insomnia and anxiety disorders. The Torture of the Cells is the chronic inflammation is the root cause of autoimmune diseases and cancer. Unforgiveness is drinking poison and expecting the other person to die.

The debt that the servant refused to release became a physical weight. By holding onto the anger, he was holding onto the stress. He became his own jailer. Dr. Everett Worthington, a pioneer in the scientific study of forgiveness, distinguishes between two types of forgiveness. **Decisional Forgiveness** is the behavioral intention to treat the person civilly and not seek revenge. You can do this with your will. **Emotional Forgiveness** is the replacement of negative, unforgiving emotions with positive, other-oriented emotions like empathy and compassion. This is the biological shift.

You can have Decisional Forgiveness without Emotional Forgiveness. You can act nice while rotting inside, but true healing requires Emotional Forgiveness. It requires the biology to change.

PART III: THE SCAPEGOAT (YOM KIPPUR)

God knew that human beings were not built to carry the toxic load of sin and betrayal forever. He knew that if we let it accumulate, it would crush us. So, in **Leviticus 16**, He established a national holiday of release called Yom Kippur, the Day of Atonement. The word *Kippur* comes from a root meaning "to cover" or "to wipe clean." It is the annual reset button for the nation of Israel.

The central ritual of this day involved two goats. The first goat was sacrificed on the altar. Its blood was used to cleanse the Holy Place. The second goat or the scapegoat was kept alive. The High Priest would lay both hands on the head of the live goat. He would confess over it all the wickedness and rebellion of the Israelites. He would symbolically transfer the "toxic load" of the entire nation onto the head of the animal.

> *The goat will carry on itself all their sins to a remote place; and the man shall release it in the wilderness.*
>
> ***-Leviticus 16:22***

This is a profound picture of somatic therapy.

God was teaching them that they could not keep this sin and bitterness in your bodies. They have to put it on something else and send it away. The Scapegoat was the carrier of the toxin. It took the shame, the guilt, and the collective grudge of the people and walked it out into the desert, never to return.

In the New Testament, Jesus becomes both goats. He is the sacrificial first goat, and the carrier in the scapegoat. As John the Baptist said: *"Look, the Lamb of God, who takes away the sin of the world!"* **John 1:29**. Forgiveness is the act of engaging the Scapegoat mechanism.

When we forgive, we are taking the "Issue in the Tissue" and we are laying it on Christ. We are saying, *"Lord, this is too heavy for me. It is rotting my bones. I am transferring it to You. Take it into the wilderness."*

To do this we have to use the release valve. We use the liquid language.

PART IV: THE ESAU PROTOCOL

The Bible gives us a dramatic case study of this biological reconciliation in the story of Jacob and Esau. This is a twenty-year grudge. It is the prototype of family dysfunction. Jacob, the deceiver, stole Esau's birthright and his blessing. Esau, the hunter, vowed to kill him. Jacob fled for his life. For two decades, they lived in a state of Cold War.

Then, in **Genesis 33**, the time comes for them to meet. Jacob is terrified. He is stuck in the Sympathetic Nervous System of fear. He expects a battle. He divides his family into groups to minimize the casualties. He sends gifts ahead to appease Esau. He bows down to the ground seven times which is the posture of submission and safety.

He is preparing for violence, but Esau, the man of war, the rough man, the man who held the grudge.

> *But Esau ran to meet Jacob and embraced him; he threw his arms around his neck and kissed him.*
> ***And they wept.***
>
> ***-Genesis 33:4***

This is the explosion of the release valve. Twenty years of tension. Twenty years of cortisol. Twenty years of rehearsing the injury, and in one moment of physical contact, with a hug, the dam breaks. They did not just shake hands. They did not just sign a treaty. They wept.

The text emphasizes the physical intimacy of running, embracing, kissing, and tears. This is the parasympathetic shift. The "Predator" became the "Brother" again. The weeping was the solvent that washed away the history. Without the tears, the reconciliation would have been political, with the tears, it was biological. They became family again. Esau engaged the scapegoat mechanism. He let the anger go into the wilderness, and he let his brother back into his heart.

PART V: SHAME VS. GUILT (THE REPAIR EFFECT)

What is the biology of the person asking for forgiveness? Is there a difference between *"I'm sorry I got caught"* and *"I'm sorry I hurt you"*?

Science says yes, and so does the Bible. The distinction lies in the difference between shame and guilt.

In **2 Corinthians 7:10**, Paul lays out a brilliant psychological taxonomy:

> *Godly sorrow brings repentance that leads to salvation and leaves no regret, but worldly sorrow brings death.*

-2 Corinthians 7:10

Let's map this onto neurobiology. Worldly sorrow corresponds to the emotion of shame. Shame is self-focused. When a person feels shame, their limbic system triggers a withdrawal response. They want to hide. They want to cover up. Adam in the garden said "I was afraid because I was naked; so I hid." The cheating spouse lie to cover their tracks, not to protect you, but to protect their own image. The biology of shame is a stressor. It spikes cortisol. It activates the "Freeze" response. This brings death because it kills connection. A person in shame runs away from the relationship. They can not be reconciled because they can not be seen. They are defensive, evasive, and numb. This is why "I'm sorry you feel that way" is not an apology. It is a shield.

Godly sorrow corresponds to the emotion of guilt or empathy. Guilt says, *"I did something bad."* Godly sorrow is other-focused. It says, *"I hurt you, and that breaks my heart."* When a person feels Godly sorrow, their brain releases oxytocin which is the bonding hormone. They experience a repair response. They want to fix the breach. Peter after denying Christ wept bitterly, but then he swam to shore to meet Jesus. He moved toward the one he hurt. The repentant spouse confesses fully. They weep for the pain they caused. They offer restitution.

Biologically, Godly Sorrow is a form of love. It is the pain of realizing you damaged the attachment. The tears of Godly Sorrow honest signal (as discussed in Chapter 4). They are blinding themselves. They are making themselves vulnerable. This signal de-escalates the victim's anger. It is very hard to stay in "Attack Mode" when the enemy is weeping and defenseless. The tears of the offender invite the tears of the victim, and the two waters mix.

This leads to a psychological phenomenon known as the Repair Effect. Relationship experts like Dr. John Gottman have found that a bond that has been broken and successfully repaired through deep repentance and forgiveness is often stronger than a bond that was never tested. The repair process releases massive amounts of oxytocin and dopamine for both parties. It wires the two brains together in a deep, secure attachment. The scar tissue is stronger than the original skin.

PART VI: THE GIFT OF TEARS

The early Church Fathers, particularly the Desert Fathers

who lived in the silence of the Egyptian and Syrian wilderness, developed a profound theology of weeping. They had a term for it: *donum lacrimarum* or the Gift of Tears.

In the modern world, we consider crying to be a "breakdown." If someone starts crying in church, we rush to hush them or get them a tissue to stop the flow. We treat it as a problem to be solved, but the Desert Fathers treated it as a charisma, like a spiritual gift, like prophecy or teaching.

St. Isaac the Syrian wrote: *"If you cannot weep, do not imagine that you can know God."* He did not mean that dry-eyed people are atheists. He meant that the knowledge of God is not an intellectual exercise. It is an intimate encounter, and you can not be intimate while your defenses are up.

The Gift of Tears was the grace to feel the truth. To feel the weight of one's own sin through repentance. To feel the depth of God's love through gratitude. To feel the sorrow of the world through compassion. They believed that a "hard heart" was a dry heart. A heart that could not cry was calcified. It was encased in pride.

When the tears finally came, it was a sign that the stone was turning back into flesh. It was a sign that the Spirit was moving. In this light, forgiveness is the ultimate exercise of the Gift of Tears. It is the moment when we allow the Spirit to liquify our defenses.

PART VII: THE REFINERY OF THE SOUL

This brings us full circle to the central metaphor of this book. We began in Chapter 1 by looking at the eye as a filtration system. We end by looking at the human soul as a refinery. A refinery is a place where raw, crude, toxic material enters, and useful, pure energy comes out.

Every day, the raw materials of a fallen world are dumped into your hopper. You ingest betrayal. You ingest rejection. You ingest the violence of the news. You ingest the grief of loss. These are the inputs. They are unavoidable. Jesus promised them: *"In this world you will have trouble."*

What is your machinery? If you have no machinery to process this raw material, if you are tearless, the material sits inside you. It stagnates. It rots. It turns into bitterness. It turns into violence. It turns into sickness. The crude oil becomes a toxic sludge that poisons the ground of your life, but God has installed a machine in the center of your being. He gave you a nervous system that can down-shift. He gave you a lacrimal gland that can excrete stress. He gave you a voice that can lament. He gave you a spirit that can forgive.

When you use the machinery, when you weep, when you fast, when you kneel, when you forgive, you are refining the crude oil. You *input* pain. You *process* it through lament and tears. You *output* praise, peace, and love.

This is the great alchemy of the Christian life. We do not deny the pain. We are not delusional. We do not drown in the pain because that is despair. We process the pain. We turn the sorrow into song. We turn the grudge into grace.

Conclusion: The Clean Vessel

The work is done. The Sackcloth has been worn. The Stomach has been emptied. The Hand has been opened. The Prayer has been groaned. The Grudge has been released.

The "torturers" have left the building. The "toxic load" has been transferred to the scapegoat. What remains is a clean vessel, a quiet mind, and a soft heart. This is the state of **Shalom**. It is the state where the Presence of God can dwell without obstruction.

This state is not the end of the story. It is a preparation for the final destination. We are not just cleaning ourselves up for the sake of hygiene, we are cleaning ourselves up for a Wedding. We are preparing to return to the place where the need for the Sackcloth ends forever. We are preparing to return to Eden.

Chapter 12:

The Return to Eden

PART I: THE GARDEN OF NO TEARS

In the beginning, there was no sackcloth. If we travel back to the opening chapters of Genesis, before the Fall, we find a world that is difficult for us to imagine. It is a world of lush vegetation and perfect order. The most important feature of Eden was the Presence of the Lord.

Genesis 3:8 describes Adam and Eve walking with God *"in the cool of the day."* The Hebrew phrase implies a habitual intimacy. There was no barrier. There was no static. The communication between the Creator and the created was unhindered. Adam did not need to fast to hear God's voice. God was right there. He did not need to lament to process his trauma. There was no trauma. He did not need to give sacrificially to break the grip of fear. There was no fear. There were no tears.

This is the biological baseline of the Kingdom of God. The human body, in its perfected state, operating in the full Presence of the Father, has no need for the liquid language.

Tears are a language of deficit. We cry because something is missing. We cry from grief because a person is missing. We cry from pain because health is missing. We cry from shame because dignity is missing. We cry from longing because home is missing. In Eden, nothing was missing. The "Shalom," or Peace, was absolute. Adam was whole. Eve was whole. The relationship was whole.

Then came the fruit, the rebellion, and the hiding. Immediately following the Fall, the sound of the world changed.

PART II: THE FIRST LAMENT (THE FATHER'S CRY)

We often think of lament as something humans do toward God. We picture ourselves crying out from the pit, begging God to answer, but the biblical pattern is actually the reverse. The first lament in human history did not come from the throat of a man. It came from the throat of God.

Genesis 3:9 (The First Lament):

But the Lord God called to the man, and said to him, 'Where are you?'

-Genesis 3:9

This is not the question of a policeman looking for a criminal because the all-knowing God knows exactly where Adam is hiding. This is the cry of a Father looking for His lost child. It is a wail of separation. It is the original "How Long?"

God was the first one to feel the agony of the broken connection. Every lament we have uttered since then is just an echo of that first divine cry. We are responding to His call. We are trying to find our way back to the Presence that asked, *"Where are you?"* The return journey is not easy. The Fall introduced a new weight to the human experience, encapsulated in a single Hebrew word: *Itsabon.*

The "Tears" (Eve's Sorrow):

I will greatly multiply your sorrow and your

> *conception; in pain (**itsabon**) you shall bring forth children.*
>
> ***-Genesis 3:16***

The "Groans" (Adam's Toil):

> *Cursed is the ground for your sake; in toil (**itsabon**) you shall eat of it all the days of your life.*
>
> ***-Genesis 3:17***

The word *itsabon* implies worry, pain, heavy labor, and hardship.

Both the bringing forth of life, in Eve, and the sustaining of life, in Adam, are now marked by this heavy, sorrowful toil. Nothing comes easily anymore, and this extends to our spiritual life. This extends to prayer.

In the Garden, talking to God was a *"cool of the day"* stroll. It was effortless, but now, in the gap, prayer is *itsabon*. It is labor. It is a wrestling match. This is why we groan. This is why we need the Sackcloth. The mechanism of connection has been damaged by the Fall, and it now requires the *"sweat of the brow"* to push through the static. We are laboring to get back to the Father who is calling our name.

PART III: LIVING IN THE GAP

We live in the "In-Between." We are the exiles carrying the weight of *itsabon*. We wake up every day in a world that is not our home. We face cancer, divorce, racism, war, and death. Our bodies are constantly absorbing the "toxic load" of a fallen planet.

This is why the "Health and Wealth" gospel is so biologically and spiritually dangerous. It tries to pretend that we are already in Eden. It tells us that if we just have enough faith, we will not get sick, we will not be sad, and prayer will always be easy.

That is a lie. We are not in Eden yet. We are in the wilderness, and in the wilderness, you need a survival strategy.

This entire book has been an instruction manual for that strategy.

We Lament: Because the world is broken, and we need to flush the debris from our hearts so we do not become hard.

We Fast: Because the world is distracting (Sodom), and we need to clear the noise so we can hear the faint signal of home.

We Give: Because the world is scary (Mammon), and we

need to unclench our fists so we do not become hoarders.

We Pray: Because the world is lonely, and we need to connect with the Father who collects our tears.

These practices are the "Brushing of the Teeth." They are the daily maintenance required to keep the vessel clean while we walk through the mud. If you stop brushing your teeth in the wilderness, you will lose them. If you stop lamenting in the wilderness, you will lose your heart.

PART IV: THE PRESENCE IS THE PRIZE

The goal is **The Presence.** Throughout history, whenever God's people practiced these things, the Presence returned. When Nineveh fasted and put on sackcloth, the judgment was lifted, and mercy (Presence) returned. When Jesus wept at Bethany, the power of God raised the dead. You must empty the vessel to fill the vessel.

You can not fill a cup that is already full of vinegar. You have to dump it out first. Lament dumps out the pain. Fasting dumps out the flesh. Giving dumps out the greed, and into that empty space, the Spirit rushes in.

This experience of the Presence is the *"peace that sur-*

passes understanding" **Philippians 4:7**. It does not mean the cancer goes away. It doesn't mean the divorce did not happen. It means that *in the middle* of the cancer, and *in the middle* of the divorce, you are not alone. You are held.

PART V: THE FINAL WIPE (THE BOTTLE AND THE BOOK)

The Bible does not end in the wilderness. It ends with a return. It ends with the resolution of all the "*Groans*" and "*Tears*" we have been studying.

In **Revelation 21**, John sees the New Jerusalem coming down out of heaven. It is the restoration of all things.

And in verse 4, we see the final destiny of the liquid language:

> *He will wipe every tear from their eyes. There will be no more death or mourning or crying or pain, for the old order of things has passed away.*
>
> ***-Revelation 21:4***

We must connect the dots here. This is the culmination of the entire theology of the Sackcloth.

The Bottle (Psalm 56:8): We learned that God collects every tear in His bottle. He values our pain. He keeps the record.

The Translator (Romans 8:26): We learned that the Spirit takes our "wordless groans" (our *itsabon*) and translates them into perfect prayers because we do not know what to say.

The Wipe (Revelation 21:4): Now, at the end of history, the bottle is opened. The record is settled. The groans are answered.

The "*wiping away*" is not just a Kleenex moment. It is the moment where the God who collected the tears finally redeems the tears. Every drop of liquid language you ever shed was a sentence in a conversation that God has been listening to your whole life. In Revelation 21, He finishes the conversation. He wipes the eyes because the *Itsabon* is over. The toil is over. The pain is over. The separation that caused the First Lament ("Where are you?") is closed forever.

We are found.

PART VI: THE CHALLENGE TO THE CRY BABY

This leaves us with a choice.

We can continue to run from our sorrow. We can continue to suppress the "cry baby" inside us. We can continue to numb ourselves with food and noise, building up a toxic load that will eventually kill us. We can continue to act "strong" while we rot on the inside.

OR, we can embrace the Sackcloth.

We can choose to view our sensitivity not as a weakness, but as a cheat code. We can choose to view our tears not as a failure, but as a prayer.

I want to speak directly to the person reading this who feels like I felt as a child. That choice to run from their tears.

Do not harden your heart.

Your softness is your greatest weapon. Your ability to feel is the proof that you are still alive in a dying world. Your tears are the evidence that you have not succumbed to the numbness of Sodom. God is not asking you to toughen up. He is asking you to open up. He is asking you to go into your room, close the door, and let the river flow. He is asking you to fast from the noise so you can hear His song. He is asking you to open your hand so you can hold His.

The Sackcloth is not a punishment. It is a portal. It is the doorway out of the headache of resistance and into the abundance of peace.

Conclusion: The Abundant Life

Jesus said,

> *I have come that they may have life, and have it to the full*
>
> ***- John 10:10.***

We often mistake "full life" for "happy life" or "easy life." A full life is a life that *feels* everything. It feels the crushing weight of Good Friday and the explosive joy of Resurrection Sunday. It feels the hunger of the fast and the satisfaction of the feast.

To live abundantly is to live with the valve open. It is to trust God with your pain as much as you trust Him with your joy. So, put on the sackcloth when the day is dark. Wash your face when the morning comes, and know that every single drop you shed is counted, collected, and cherished by the God who loves you.

He is coming. He is bringing a handkerchief. But until then... let it flow.

Sources Cited

Biblical Texts

All scripture quotations, unless otherwise indicated, are taken from the Holy Bible, New International Version®, NIV®. Copyright ©1973, 1978, 1984, 2011 by Biblica, Inc.™ Used by permission of Zondervan. All rights reserved worldwide.

Key Passages Referenced:

Genesis 3:8-19 (The Fall, The First Lament, *Itsabon*)

Genesis 4:1-16 (Cain and Abel, The rejection of lament leading to violence)

Genesis 33:1-11 (Jacob and Esau, The reconciliation through weeping)

Leviticus 16 (The Day of Atonement, The Scapegoat)

1 Samuel 21:10-15 (David feigning madness in Gath)

2 Samuel 1:11-12 (David fasting and weeping for Saul)

Psalm 6:6 (The physical exhaustion of grief)

Psalm 13 (The architecture of lament: Scream, Silence, Shift, Song)

Psalm 56:8 (Tears in a bottle, The Book of Remembrance)

Proverbs 4:23 (Guarding the heart)

Ecclesiastes 7:2-4 (The House of Mourning vs. The House of Feasting)

Isaiah 58:1-12 (True Fasting vs. False Fasting)

Ezekiel 16:49-50 (The sin of Sodom: Overfed and Unconcerned)

Daniel 1, 9, 10 (The diet vs. the spiritual fast)

Matthew 6:1-18 (Giving, Prayer, and Fasting in secret)

Matthew 19:16-22 (The Rich Young Ruler)

Matthew 25:31-46 (The Sheep and the Goats)

John 11:1-44 (The raising of Lazarus, Jesus weeping)

Romans 8:26-27 (The Spirit interceding with wordless groans)

Revelation 21:1-4 (The New Jerusalem, The wiping of tears)

Scientific & Medical References

Frey, William H. II. *Crying: The Mystery of Tears.* Winston Press, 1985. (Source for the chemical composition of emotional tears vs. reflex tears, specifically ACTH and Manganese).

Vingerhoets, Ad. *Why Only Humans Weep: Unravelling the Mysteries of Tears.* Oxford University Press, 2013. (Source for the Parasympathetic function of crying).

Van der Kolk, Bessel. *The Body Keeps the Score: Brain, Mind, and Body in the Healing of Trauma.* Viking, 2014. (Source for Broca's Area shutdown during trauma and somatic memory).

Gottman, John M., and Silver, Nan. *The Seven Principles for Making Marriage Work.* Harmony, 1999. (Source for the "Repair Effect" in relationships).

Moll, J., et al. "Human Fronto-Mesolimbic Networks Guide Decisions about Charitable Donation." *Proceedings of the National Academy of Sciences*, 2006. (Source for the neurological "Helper's High" and oxytocin release during giving).

Sapolsky, Robert M. *Why Zebras Don't Get Ulcers.* W.H. Freeman, 2004. (Source for the physiology of stress, cortisol, and the Autonomic Nervous System).

James, Sherman A. "John Henryism and the Health of African Americans." *Culture, Medicine and Psychiatry*, 1994. (Source for the "John Henry Effect" and health disparities in the Black community).

Historical & Psychological Concepts

The Hydraulic Model of Aggression: A psychological theory suggesting that unexpressed emotion builds pressure that must be released, often resulting in violence if healthy channels are blocked. (Reference: Freud, S., and later adaptations by Konrad Lorenz).

Alexithymia: A personality construct characterized by the subclinical inability to identify and describe emotions in the self. (Reference: Sifneos, Peter E., 1973).

Embodied Cognition: The theory that many features of cognition, whether human or otherwise, are shaped by aspects of the entire body of the organism. (Reference: Varela, Thompson, and Rosch, *The Embodied Mind*, 1991).

The Desert Fathers: Early Christian monastics (3rd-4th century AD) who developed the concept of *donum lacrimarum* (The Gift of Tears). Reference specifically St. Isaac the Syrian.

Gilligan, James. *Violence: Our Deadly Epidemic and Its Causes.* G.P. Putnam's Sons, 1996. (Source for the connection between unacknowledged shame and violence).

www.ingramcontent.com/pod-product-compliance
Lightning Source LLC
LaVergne TN
LVHW090610110826
845146LV00001B/323

* 9 7 9 8 9 9 5 5 0 7 7 0 3 *